Astrology &
Your Destiny

Astrology & Your Destiny

discover your place in the universe through
the ancient arts of prediction and divination

Sally Morningstar • Richard Craze
Staci Mendoza • David Bourne

southwater

This edition is published by Southwater, an imprint of Anness Publishing Ltd,
Blaby Road, Wigston, Leicestershire LE18 4SE; info@anness.com

www.southwaterbooks.com; www.annesspublishing.com

Anness Publishing has a new picture agency outlet for images
for publishing, promotions or advertising. Please visit our website
www.practicalpictures.com for more information.

Publisher: Joanna Lorenz
Managing Editor: Helen Sudell
Project Editors: Emma Gray and Debra Mayhew
Designer: Axis Design
Photographers: Don Last and John Freeman
Production Controller: Wendy Lawson
Illustrator: Anna Koska

PUBLISHER'S NOTE
Although the advice and information in this book are believed to be accurate and true at the time of
going to press, neither the authors nor the publisher can accept any legal responsibility or liability for
any errors or omissions that may have been made nor for any inaccuracies nor for any loss, harm or
injury that comes about from following instructions or advice in this book.

The publishers would like to thank the following picture libraries for supplying pictures for use in this
book: A–Z Botanical Collection Ltd: 27TL; 27TR; 27ML; 27MR; AKG Photo: 13T; 14T; 14B; 15T; 15B;
16T; 16B; 17T; 17B; 18T; 19T; 19B; 91T; 91B; The Art Archive: 12T; 38T; 41T; BBC Natural History
Unit: 20T; 46TL; 46TR; Bridgeman Art Library: 6; Fine Art Photographic Library Ltd: 22T; 90T; 92B;
Galaxy Picture Library: 37BM; Garden Picture Library: 26; Images Colour Library: 6B; 7B; 12B; 21T; 42;
46MR; 93T; Planet Earth Pictures: 94TR; Stock Market: 74; Superstock: 30TL; 36T; 36B; Tony Stone
Images: 22T; 23; 25T; 34TL; 34TR; 34TML; 34TMR; 34BML; 34BMR; 34BL; 34BR; 35TR; 35TM; 35BM;
35B; 37T; 37BL; 37BR; 39T; 39B; 44BT; 44BR; 44B; 44BC; 46ML; 46BL; 46BR; 47 TL; 47TR; 47ML; 47BL;
47BR; 51T; 55B; 57T; 59TL; 61T; 63T; 65T; 67T; 69T; 71T; 73T; 75; 76T; 78T; 80T; 85B; 87; 95TL; 95B.

contents

destiny

introduction

Like a great over-arching roof, the sky seemed to ancient observers to encompass and enclose everything on earth. Beneath its giant canopy hung the sun, the moon and the stars, watching over the world as they moved across the sky. From the earliest times, human communities have learnt to watch the movements of these great heavenly bodies and to chart their regular paths, coming to understand something of their power and influence over the earth. In the following pages, we discover some of the secrets of the universe, how to harness the moon's magic, and the arts of astrology and palmistry. This practical guide can help you to understand the mystical influences on your life and to make positive choices that can only come from self-awareness and inner knowledge.

celestial intuition

The wisdom of the ancient seers lay in their understanding of the connectedness of all things. They knew that human beings are not isolated specks adrift in a vast and alien universe, but an integral part of creation, whose lives are governed and determined by the complex, interacting forces surrounding them. Through detailed watching and recording of natural events, the movement of the stars and the phases of the moon, they saw through the seemingly arbitrary events of human life to discover patterns that lay at its heart. Their growing understanding of such great designs allowed them not only to explain events but ultimately to predict them.

This huge body of knowledge has passed down from generation to generation, being refined and expanded over at least 9,000 years, to the present day. In some ages and in some civilizations, divination has formed a staple part of orthodox religion; at other times it has been suppressed, surviving only in the minds of those who knew the ancient ways. Divination is deeply embedded in all human cultures, however, and as the modern world becomes increasingly alienated from awareness of natural forces and universal mysteries, people long more and more to get back in touch with this knowledge.

This book offers a grounding in the ancient knowledge, helping you to understand, for example, how the magic of the moon influences your moods and your relationships. It shows you how your birth date pinpointed on an astrological chart, or the lines on

the palm of your hand, act like maps to guide you through your strengths and weaknesses and so assist in developing your understanding of who you are.

The influence of our nearest celestial neighbour, the moon, remains mysterious. Just as she governs the rising and falling of the tides, she exerts her gravitational pull on the fluid elements within us, affecting the rhythms of our bodies. Even those with only a passing interest in astrology will know their sun sign, but the position of the moon in the astrological chart is also important, because while the sun's position at birth influences an individual's personality, the moon governs the feelings and emotions – the secret, inner person.

lunar planetary astrology divination

wisdom
fate
palmistry

The moon has been worshipped as a goddess by many civilizations throughout history. Her ever-changing state is reflected in the three faces of the ancient Triple Goddess – maiden, mother and crone – as well as in the different aspects of the female character. The moon's special affinity with women means that an understanding of her rhythm and influence can offer new insights into women's natural physical and emotional cycles. The lunar festivals of the year affirm and celebrate life, fertility and regeneration: the vital aspects of earthly existence over which the moon reigns. Her influence over the fertility

and growth of plants can be harnessed to ensure an abundant harvest. Colours, crystals, talismans and numerology can all help to put you in touch with the magic of the moon.

The movements of the planets among the constellations create patterns and correspondences that have been observed by astrologers from the earliest times. As they became able to predict the alignments of the stars, they also discovered the subtle relationships between the stars and human nature. The regular patterns of the heavens were divided into sectors, or houses, which governed different aspects of human development and behaviour.

In China, astrological influences were ordered with reference to Taoist philosophy, with its emphasis on constant change and flux. Each birth year comes under the influence of a particular element, and the sectors of the Chinese zodiac are named after animals, who also govern the months and hours of birth, giving each person a unique horoscope.

Though astrology cannot foretell your future, it can show you a detailed picture of yourself and your potential, to enable you to make more informed choices in your life.

Palmistry is another method of divination which helps you to see yourself more clearly, but it does so by examining your physical characteristics. As you change, so do the lines on your hand. They are not fixed, and show that the future is yours in the making. A palm-reader can give you an idea of when events and situations may take place, but you can influence the course of your life and change your destiny, if you act consciously from a place of inner knowing.

moon magic
moon magic

moon magic

The moon is mysterious. She is known by many names and is worshipped by many cultures throughout the world, both ancient and modern. Our great Mother Moon inspires wonder when we see her silver light shining upon the shadows of the night. Both men and women are intimately linked to her changing faces of crescent, full, waning and dark, as she progresses through her lunar cycle. When she pulls and tugs at the waters of the earth, creating high and low tides, she also pulls at the water within our bodies, affecting our moods, sleep patterns, health, and women's "moontime" cycles. It is well documented that the full moon has powerful effects upon human mental and emotional stability.

Because the moon is within the gravitational field of the earth, her interaction with us affects weather patterns around the world. Rainfall, tropical storms, hurricanes and earthquakes have all been associated with lunar influence and acitvity. The moon is intimately linked to our world and we are deeply affected by her, as is the planet we inhabit.

By discovering some of her magical mysteries, you can get to know her better and come to understand the complex nature of her rhythms and cycles. The moon is the personification of female wisdom, the wisdom of intuitive knowledge and deep instincts. She cannot be tamed by rational thought; she is a free spirit.

lunar wisdom

Though the moon is the close companion of the earth, she retains many mysteries, and her origin is still unknown. She is, however, thought to be about 4,600 million years old, the same age as the earth. Her power was recognized in ancient cultures. She was depicted as both the giver and the taker of life, and many legends surrounding the creation concerned the complementary powers of the sun and the moon.

Facts

The moon measures 3476km/2160 miles across and her gravity is one-sixth that of the earth. The craters on the moon, which measure up to 240km/150 miles across, may be the result of impacts from comets and asteroids over millions of years, or may stem from volcanic activity within the moon itself. Humans first landed on the moon in 1969, but with hardly any atmosphere and no water, it is not possible for the moon to sustain life as we know it.

Because of the moon's elliptical orbit, she can be anything between 356,398km/221,466 miles and 406,698km/252,722 miles away from earth. This orbit pattern also means that we only ever get to see one side of her. Surface temperatures range from -233°C/-387°F at night to 127°C/260°F at midday, as the light of the sun is reflected back from the moon's surface to earth. A moon–sun conjunction creates the image of the crescent, or new, moon and a full moon occurs when the sun and moon are in alignment with each other. The moon is slowly pulling away from the earth's gravitational influence, by 3cm/1½ in annually, so the length of our daily cycle is actually increasing by a miniscule amount each year.

This limestone relief depicts Nanna, the Assyrian moon god, crowned with a crescent moon.

Legends

Because of her ever-changing and yet regenerative cycle, the moon was seen as immortal and as the place to which souls departed at death. She could bring gentle rain, but could also raise storms and ruin crops, so she was considered unpredictable and potentially destructive. Moon goddesses were endowed with both destructive and creative powers. The Mayans' moon deity was called Ixchel, and was feared as the bringer of floods and storms. Her skirt was decorated with bones, and her crown was a serpent. Despite this she was also a protector of women in childbirth.

In Sumerian mythology, the principal moon deity, Sin, was male. He was associated with the new moon and was responsible for the fertility of the land, for food production and the protection of herds, especially cattle. The re-enactment of the sacred marriage between the male (waxing) and female (waning) aspects of the lunar cycle was undertaken between the king of Ur, embodying the god Sin, and the goddess in the person of a priestess. By performing this ceremony, they were enacting the continuance and co-operation of the two opposites.

In Native American mythology, the spider, who has universal links with the moon, was the weaver of the web of creation, producing the physical world, and then supporting and nurturing life on earth. The snail, because of its moisture trail and its seeming ability to vanish and reappear, is also linked to the moon. It was thought that the snail could travel into the underworld and re-emerge unharmed. The Mexican moon god, Tecciztecatl, was depicted in the shell of a snail.

Mirrors figure prominently in moon lore, because of their reflective qualities, and have long been used for divination. In 19th-century Britain it was common for girls to use a mirror and the full moon to find out when they would be married. Two and a half thousand years earlier, it is said that Pythagoras was taught mirror divination by the wise woman of Thessaly.

Some believe that the moon and the earth were once a single planet, others that the moon was drawn into the earth's force field at some point. Yet another hypothesis is that the two planets were formed together out of the same space dust and cosmic gases. The actual origin of the moon remains a mystery.

moon worship

Many ancient civilizations venerated the moon because they witnessed her regenerative powers, saw how she influenced the growth of crops, how she matched the average female menstrual cycle, and how she affected weather. Even her dark time was seen to hold secrets about death and the veil that separates spirit from matter. She seemed to hold the key to deep and profound wisdom about the rhythms and cycles of existence.

Goddesses

Because it was important to differentiate between the phases of the moon, different goddesses represented them. The Greeks, for example, worshipped Artemis as the new moon, Selene as the full moon and Hecate as the waning moon. In Rome, Artemis became Diana. The cult of Isis, the Egyptian "Good Mother", spread through Greece and Rome and was eventually absorbed by the cult of the Virgin Mary, also a lady of the moon.

So strong was the compulsion to honour the moon goddess and keep her favour, that sacrifices and orgiastic rites were regularly performed to appease her. All phases of the moon held secrets about the circle of life. By worshipping the appropriate goddess, humankind could try to tame her influence on such issues as pregnancy, agriculture or divination.

The dual powers of creation were represented by Isis and Osiris.

Angels

As the Great Mother, the moon has considerable influence over her "children" – angels. The angel associated with the moon is Gabriel, the healer. He is the Angel of the Annunciation, who visited the Virgin Mary (a lady of the moon). He is sometimes depicted carrying white lilies, the flowers of the Virgin, and is intimately linked with healing and with alleviating suffering on earth.

On the lunar wheel Gabriel stands in the west, in the position of the waning moon. This direction is represented by the water element. Stand facing west during a waning moon (especially if it is in a water sign) to say prayers for healing. You should also face west if you are making a water offering, which can be anything that is taken from the waters, such as watercress, a river stone, seaweed or a shell.

An Angel Healing

Perform this ceremony just after a full moon to seek healing for someone who is sick. Camphor, eucalyptus and sandalwood are all linked to the healing qualities of the moon. Write down the name of the person requiring healing, and their ailment, fold the paper twice and hold it while you say: "Angel Gabriel I ask for your help. Please bring your healing touch to [name]. By divine will, remove [this condition] from [name], for the highest good of all." End by giving thanks and blowing out the candles.

You will need

- 2 light blue candles
- white lilies
- water offering
- aromatherapy burner
- clear quartz crystal
- 9 drops of eucalyptus, sandalwood or camphor oil
- 9 white nightlights
- matches
- pen with silver ink
- natural paper
- heatproof container

1 Arrange candles, flowers, water offering and burner. Place the crystal in the water.

2 Place the nightlights in a circle around the other ingredients and light them.

3 Write your message and, holding it in your hand, ask Gabriel for his help.

4 Burn the paper in the candle flame, visualizing the ailment being carried away.

moon signs

In astrology, the position of the sun at birth represents your outer personality, whereas the position of the moon indicates your inner world of feelings and emotions. To discover the position of the moon at your birth, you will need to consult an astrologer for a natal chart. Once this has been established, you can refer to the information in the relevant section below.

When the moon is transiting Aries, there will be an increase in fiery energy, leading to the potential for confrontations.

Moon in Aries

Aries moon people tend to be impulsive and hasty, and often make quick (and sometimes rash) decisions. Their impulsiveness can make them impatient, and increase the probability of accidents. They have agile minds and are natural leaders, but need to guard against being bossy, arrogant, or dismissive of others.

Aries moons crave independence and can feel very trapped by possessive or jealous behaviour. They do not understand the depths of emotions or feel particularly comfortable with them. As this is a fire moon, their feelings are very self-orientated.

They are forward thinkers, inspired by new opportunities, wanting to carve their own path through life. People with their moon in Aries will be innovators in business, but because of their "go it alone" attitude, Aries moons can sometimes be insensitive and thoughtless. They will often regret things that they have said or done through lack of sensitivity and will then try to make up for it.

> **Stones:**
> diamond, bloodstone
> **Flower:**
> wild rose
> **Animal:**
> ram

Moon in Taurus

People with their moon in Taurus are easy-going and generally fun to be with. They appreciate fine art, music and the creative arts as well as good food and entertaining. These people are sensualists, with a love of beautiful things. They can, however, have a tendency to get stuck in ritual and routine. They dislike change and will not be pushed into anything. Above all, they are practical and down-to-earth.

Taurus moons are careful with money. Being materialistic, they like to buy good quality products and will work hard to be able to afford them. This moon's message is that life is for enjoying, but they must guard against becoming addicted to rich and unhealthy foods.

Taurus moons can feel very threatened by challenges to family life, and will do anything to maintain security. Their possessiveness can sometimes be stifling for others.

> **Stone:**
> emerald
> **Flower:**
> rose
> **Animal:**
> bull

When the moon is passing through Taurus, be careful with your possessions. Take care of personal finances and practical matters.

When the moon is transiting Gemini it is an important time to make sure that everything is based on fact, not to get carried away, and to guard against being too flippant about responsibilities. Be aware that stress will be an issue during this time, with an increase in the possibility of nervous tension and exhaustion.

Moon in Gemini

People with their moon in Gemini are mentally agile, flitting from one idea to another with ease. They have many projects on the go and need to learn to complete what they begin. Gemini moons can be gossips and chatterboxes, because of their love of the spoken word (and the sound of their own voices). The greatest challenges for Gemini moons are an appreciation of silence and consolidation of actions.

Boredom sets in quickly because their minds are constantly thinking up better ideas or solutions to problems. Their quickwittedness and versatility is therefore a strength as well as a potential weakness. Because of their tendency to move on quickly (unless the conversation is fascinating), they often miss opportunities to learn from, or understand, others.

Gemini moons find emotional people difficult to be around, and often have difficulty expressing their own feelings. They are drawn to the lighter side of life, where chatting and social interaction prevail. As long as they have stimulating outlets for their inspirations and sociability, they will be happy and content.

Gemini parents like to stimulate the minds of their children, providing them with opportunities for exploration. They find it difficult to remain constant but are fun to be with and will spend hours at play with their family.

Stone:
agate
Flower:
lavender
Animal:
monkey

Moon in Cancer

The moon is exalted in Cancer. This means that she is in her best placement here. The moon governs this zodiacal sign and so will be a powerful influence. Cancer moon people are highly sensitive and crave emotional security. They need to be accepted for who they are, so they can become extremely defensive when challenged. They are sensitive to atmospheres and are very intuitive. Their feelings are often correct, but they need to guard against presuming they are correct all the time, falling into the negative trap of feeling wronged, hurt or rejected.

Cancer moon people are the carers of the zodiac, taking on the sick and the weak. This gives them the opportunity to excel in what they do best, but this caring should not be allowed to spill over into obsessional behaviour. They must learn to let others make their own mistakes and try not to rescue everyone they perceive is in need. They can be possessive and clingy, often retreating from areas of conflict instead of discussing them. They have a tendency towards self pity and sometimes have a moody and unpredictable side. They often expect the worst.

Cancer moon women can suffer more than most from pre-menstrual tension.

Stone:
moonstone
Flower:
waterlily
Animal:
crab

Cancer moon people make caring and supportive parents. When the moon is transiting Cancer, it is a good time to spend with the family, or helping others. Try to avoid depressing situations.

Moon in Leo

People with their moon in Leo are naturally gregarious and love being the centre of attention. They know little fear and will have a go at most things, believing that everything is attainable. They may tend to be bossy and self-centred, but this is a double-edged tendency, because they can also be great motivators to others who lack their level of confidence. They need to ensure that they find ways to balance their extrovert side with steadying activities that slow them down a little.

Above all, Leo moons need to be recognized and appreciated. Like the lioness, Leo moon people are proud and able. They love romance, and may often have a string of admirers who adore them. It is important to learn humility when your moon is in Leo and to sprinkle this over a naturally flamboyant lifestyle.

Caution is not the strongest characteristic when the moon is placed here. Think before you act, and plan before you begin, otherwise several very creative ideas may get lost in a whirl of self-aggrandizement. Leo moons are sociable and enjoy mixing with others. As parents, they see their children as extensions of their own egos, and so will push them to succeed. This pressure can drive a child away early from the home, if levels of control or domination are just too overwhelming.

Stone:
ruby
Flower:
sunflower
Animal:
lion

When the moon is transiting Leo, you need to guard against being self-centred, over-opinionated or pushy.

When the moon is transiting Virgo, issues surrounding health and exercise will arise. This is a good time to begin a new fitness plan.

Moon in Virgo

Moon in Virgo people are discriminating, exacting and extremely clean and tidy. They are tactful and diplomatic, so make excellent peacemakers and negotiators.

Virgo moon people tend to be nervous and highly strung, lacking a basic confidence. Their way with words can sometimes be wonderful, and writers often have their moon in this sign. They need to guard against being too critical or judgemental: their high standards and expectations can make others feel inadequate or uncomfortable. They excel in most things they attempt, because they are methodical in their approach. Their attention to detail means that their homes are spotless, their offices organized, and all plans are made with care, leaving little room for error. This strictness can be limiting sometimes, and learning a level of flexibility and fluidity can, therefore, be highly beneficial.

Virgo moons are steady and reliable partners, good at handling and investing money. They approach parenting as they do everything else — with orderly correctness — and everything is taken care of in a practical way. However, paranoia about mess can cause friction in the family and Virgo moon parents need to learn to loosen up and allow their children the freedom to get dirty once in a while.

Stone:
jade
Flower:
buttercup
Animal:
cat

Moon in Libra

Moon in Libra people love beauty and harmony. They are naturally charming and likeable, and are able to see an argument from many different points of view. This makes them excellent lawyers, diplomats, or politicians. Ultimately, however, the final decision-making is quite distasteful to them.

Stone:
opal
Flower:
violet
Animal:
hare

They are understanding and sensitive to the thoughts and feelings of others, which means that they can often be used as a shoulder to cry on. But other people would be wise to understand that the Libra moon's sensitivity can also be withdrawn if it is taken for granted or seen as a weakness.

Being naturally creative, their homes are artistically decorated and put together, even if little money is available. This artistic streak can also extend into their working lives, with a job in the performing or visual arts, such as theatre, painting, dance or music.

They fall in love easily and enjoy their relationships, having a need to relate to other people. They must, however, avoid escapism and learn to face up to their own faults. Disharmony in the home can lead quite quickly to ill health, producing headaches and physical tension.

Libra parents want to share their cultured interests with their children, but they need to allow their offspring to develop their own identity, follow their own particular talents and allow their creativity to shine however they choose.

Moon in Libra people create lovely homes with relaxing environments. When the moon is passing through Libra it is a good time to focus upon harmony within relationships.

When the moon is passing through Scorpio, destructive attitudes are possible. This is not the time to talk about sensitive issues.

Moon in Scorpio

People with their moon in Scorpio will be intensely secretive and difficult to fathom, and any hurts will be stored away for a long, long time. The light-hearted side of life often escapes them, and they are sometimes much too serious..

Stone:
topaz
Flower:
chrysanthemum
Animal:
eagle

This can lead to addictive patterns of behaviour. Scorpio moons need to learn how to channel their feelings into such things as self-healing, team games, and a healthy routine. They can, however, utilize their intuitive skills in medicine, research, healing and detective work, and they are happiest when left to get on with a task quietly.

In relationships, they have a lot to give, if they will let go enough to give it. They should not bear grudges or carry hurt feelings for too long, but learn how to forgive and move on.

Scorpio moon parents are fiercely protective of their offspring, sometimes bordering on possessiveness and jealousy, and do not welcome advice. They need to understand that children need a diversity of relationships in order to develop a well-rounded sociability. Any over-protectiveness is extremely supportive when necessary, but stifling when it is not.

When the moon is passing through Sagittarius, things may not go according to plan. It is a time to be adaptable.

Moon in Sagittarius

Sagittarius moon people are gregarious, funny, witty and tactless. Often speaking without thinking, these people need to learn how to be sociable without putting their foot in it. They are highly independent and individualistic, not worrying too much about what others think of them, since they hold quite a high opinion of their own abilities anyway.

They are very able, but a lack of sensitivity can sometimes mean that they tread on other people as they climb or travel to the top. They rise to a challenge, but need to guard against carelessness, including carelessness with money. Gambling is a strong temptation. Sagittarius moons can be reckless and would benefit from learning to pay attention to detail.

They have a naturally carefree attitude, which sometimes borders upon restlessness if their intellect is not sufficiently stimulated. Their work needs to be challenging, so that they can rise to the task. This moon placement can bring great wisdom, if the carefree attitude is tempered with sensibility.

They make good partners and are probably among the best parents in the zodiac. However, if things start to go wrong in a relationship you will not see Sagittarians for dust. They will have left already, looking for a more optimistic landscape. Generally happy people, they find it hard to stay where they feel uncomfortable.

Stone:
sapphire
Flower:
carnation
Animal:
horse

Moon in Capricorn

People with their moon in Capricorn will be hard-working, perhaps even workaholics. They have an almost fanatical dedication to making money and becoming successful, often at the expense of personal relationships. This placement is not an easy one, and lunar Capricorns often have to make sacrifices, which can lead them to become martyrs, with a tendency to moan about their lot. Capricorn moons can suffer with allergies and skin complaints, and benefit from being spontaneous, especially when the limitations of martyrdom are affecting their health.

Women with their moon in Capricorn often put their feelings aside and settle with a partner who will provide them with material security. Men, on the other hand, will often connect with a woman who can further their career. This is not a sign that is willing to take risks. Emotions do not figure strongly with Capricorn moons, and there can be a tendency to aloofness and detachment. This is sometimes balanced with a warm and funny sense of humour which rises spontaneously and can help to balance the rather superior, rigid exterior so often presented to the world.

Stone:
onyx
Flower:
pansy
Animal:
goat

When the moon is passing through Capricorn, it is a good time to work on your finances, and attend to any practical matters. Capricorn men and women set great store by financial security.

Moon in Aquarius

People with the moon in Aquarius can be highly original thinkers and extremely creative, often following a career in the performing or creative arts. They are interesting and unusual, and have many fascinated friends. However, Aquarius moons must guard against careless talk or flippant actions at times when life is too dull or humdrum for them. They need to find a balance between innovative ideas and practical actions, and to avoid getting carried away with the next brilliant brainwave before it proves to be workable. They are outspoken and inventive. As lovers of freedom, they are often drawn to improving society in some way. Their need for independence runs deep, and Aquarius moons hate to be tied down. They frequently present mysterious and magnetic qualities that draw the unusual to them. They can be secretive and difficult to fathom because of this rather enigmatic predisposition.

Aquarius moons are unpredictable, never quite reacting as expected, and sometimes causing confusion as a result. They need to ensure that they stay well grounded in material matters and in business concerns. Nervous tension can affect their health adversely, especially the eyes and lower body.

Moon in Aquarius parents are double-sided. They give strong moral support to their children, but also expect them to become independent at a young age.

Stone:
jet
Flower:
snowdrop
Animal:
swallow

When the moon is passing through Aquarius, there will be an increase in creative and metaphysical ideas, with the opportunity to perform charitable acts. This is a good time to have a party.

When the moon is passing through Pisces, guard against emotional outbursts or negative and depressive tendencies.

Moon in Pisces

Stone:
amethyst
Flower:
mosses
Animal:
fish

People with their moon in Pisces are extremely sensitive, and often psychic, with a natural intuitive ability. They are kind, compassionate and understanding. There is also a creative streak in lunar Pisceans, and once they have gained confidence in their abilities, they have the potential to be extremely successful. They see life as far more than material, and give a great deal to those in need.

However, they can also be dishonest, out of a fear of conflict. Piscean moons can tend to put things off, making all kinds of excuses, but with the right kind of encouragement, they have the ability to make a great contribution to society.

Being romantic by nature, they require strong and positive partners, who will understand the Piscean sensitivity and vulnerability, and who will give back as much as they contribute to any partnership. It is easy to abuse the goodwill of Piscean moons, or to misunderstand their deep emotional nature.

Piscean parents are kind and sensitive to their children's needs, but sometimes lean on them for support.

the lunar year
Ancient civilizations calculated their festivals according to the lunar cycles of the year. Our present Gregorian calendar is calculated according to the position of the earth in relation to the sun – measuring the length of a solar day – rather than by the far less predictable monthly cycle of the moon. Although it is more complicated, many cultures, such as the Hebrews and Muslims, still have the means to calculate time by the moon.

Lunar Festivals

A lunar year is calculated by months rather than days, each incorporating the new, full, waning and dark aspects of the moon. For Buddhists, who use a lunar calendar, full and new moons are very important times, because they believe that Buddha was born, achieved enlightenment and died during the period of the full moon. Several of our solar festivals were originally lunar festivals, hence their appearance in the lunar wheel of the year. Easter still coincides with a particular full moon. The Celtic celebrations of Imbolc (1 February) and Beltane (1 May) were also dedicated to the moon.

Some days are dedicated to moon goddesses. One of Diana's festivals is called the Ides of May, and falls at the time of the May full moon. At this time, women would clean and tidy grottos, streams and water holes, and then wash the water over themselves as an act of cleansing and to encourage personal fertility. Diana is also venerated at the Harvest moon. Hecate, a moon goddess of the dark aspect, has her annual festival day on 13 August. This is the time when ancient peoples would call for her blessing on fair weather for a safe harvest.

The moon is honoured in many cultures. Zhong Qiu Jie is an autumnal lunar festival held by the Chinese, when offerings are made and celebrations abound to honour a bountiful harvest. The lunar cycle is celebrated by pagans in the form of "full moon esbats". These ceremonies involve celebrating the full moon and sharing a feast, after any requests or dedications have been made, to signify the great abundance of the mother aspect of the moon and her ripeness at the full phase, being the most powerfully fertile. In many ancient cultures, torches were lit to direct the rays of the moon down to the earth, to ensure her continued influence upon crops, childbirth, and fair weather.

The Celts often lit ceremonial fires when the moon rose on the evening before the day of a festival.

Lunar Festivals of the Year

30 November eve	Festival of Hecate: weather	1 May	Beltane/May Day: fertility, warmth and light
20/21 December eve	Winter Solstice – Celtic festival of the stars: light and life	9 May	Festival of Artemis
31 January eve	Imbolc: rejuvenation, fertility	26–31 May	Diana's Ides of May: fertility, abundance
7 February	Festival of Selene	21 June eve	Festival of Ceridwen
12 February	Festival of Diana	13 August eve	Festival of Hecate: torchlit procession; weather and thanksgiving
15 March	Festival of Cybele		
20 March	Festival of Isis	September full moon eve	Festival of Candles/Harvest moon: crop yield
20 March eve	Festival of Eostre (Easter): fertility	31 October eve	Festival of Hecate: remembrance of ancestors
31 March	Festival of all Lunar Goddesses		

lunar phases
Traditionally, the moon has four phases: new, full, waning and dark. In ancient civilizations, the moon was considered to have three faces: the crescent, the full and the waning/dark. These three faces were embodied in the maiden, mother and crone of the Triple Goddess. Ancient tribal ceremonies, although led by the chief, were always presided over by women, who were considered the potentizers of the moon's energy.

The New Moon
Associated with Artemis, the new moon heralds the beginning of a new cycle, and is the time in magic when new opportunities can be called for. On the magic circle, the new moon is placed in the east – the place of the moonrise and the place of a rising dawn. This slender beauty is seen as young and vulnerable, filled with the potential of a full moon yet to come, but as yet unrealized. The new moon is the maiden, the innocent, the conception, and this is a good time to work on health and personal growth, and to put plans into action for the month ahead. The new moon time lasts for approximately three days of the first quarter.

The first quarter of the moon's cycle begins with the new moon, and lasts until half the moon is visible.

The first quarter is a time of expansion, development and growth, and can still be used for the same purposes as the new moon, as long as you have completed your groundwork.

The Full Moon
The full moon is the moon at her fullest and ripest. Represented by Isis, Selene, and Diana, amongst others, she is the embodiment of fertility, abundance and illumination. She is the moon at her most powerfully feminine and so is the fruit-bearer, the one who can encourage any seeds to grow. The full moon can be called upon to give fertility in the fields as well as fertility of the body, and safe journeys across water. The most potent time for full moon magic occurs in the three days prior to a full moon and at the actual time of the full moon. This is called the second quarter.

In full moon ceremonies, the high priestess draws down the energies of a full moon into herself, embodying the great mystery of the feminine, by adopting the pentagram position within a sacred circle she has cast. Having drawn down the energies, she can be filled and refreshed, so that she can complete the next cycle of events in her life and the life of her community.

The full moon is also well known as the time of moon madness, or "lunacy" (from luna, the moon). The powerful energy of a full moon can trigger such things as epilepsy, as well as increasing the potential for accidents. People vulnerable to the influence of the full moon will feel more emotionally or mentally shaky at this time. In the female reproductive cycle, the full moon is the time of ovulation.

The Waning/Dark Moon
The waning and dark moon is ruled by Hecate, Cybele and Ceridwen. The waning moon, the third quarter, is when things can be released and insights gained. This is the power time for healings. After this period, the moon enters the rising power time of the fourth quarter. This is a necessary part of the circle of Luna, when things can retreat into themselves and rest before the pull of the new moon draws everything out again.

The dark moon is the time of black magic, especially during the winter months, when the light is low. However, it is the most potent time for gaining understanding, and should ideally be spent in contemplation and meditation, seeking the spiritual guidance of Isis or of Sophia, holy lady of wisdom. Dark moon is not the time for action unless it is of a banishing nature, and this is best done during the waning moon, the first to fourth day after the full moon, and not on the nights of true darkness, unless you know what you are doing.

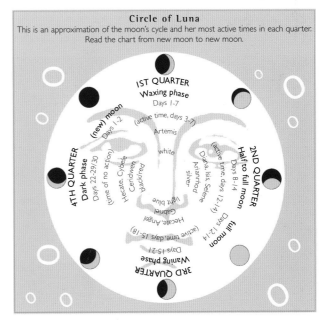

Circle of Luna
This is an approximation of the moon's cycle and her most active times in each quarter. Read the chart from new moon to new moon.

1ST QUARTER
Waxing phase
Days 1-7
(new) moon
Days 1-2
(active time, days 3-7)
Artemis
white

2ND QUARTER
Half to full moon
Days 8-14
(active time, days 12-14)
Diana, Isis, Selene
Arianrhod
silver
full moon
Days 12-14

3RD QUARTER
Waning phase
Days 15-21
(active time, days 15-18)
Hecate, Angel
Gabriel
light blue

4TH QUARTER
Dark phase
Days 22-29/30
(time of no action)
Hecate, Cybele
Ceridwen
black/red

The exact length of a lunar month is 29 days, 12 hours, 44 minutes and 28 seconds.

the influence of the moon

Before the advent of calendars, the king (or "moonman") was responsible for watching the moon's cycle and informing the tribal members when the new moon arrived, so that activities associated with the crescent could begin. Ancient people were well aware of the profound influence the moon had on their lives, influencing the weather and the tides and reflecting the natural cycles of fertility.

The Moon and Women

As the protector and guardian of women, the moon has long been associated with the female reproductive cycle. Many ancient civilizations performed fertility rituals and celebrated the moon at annual festivals dedicated to the goddess, to seek her help and favour with conception.

The female menstrual cycle mirrors the cycle of the moon in duration. The Latin word "mens" meaning both mind and moon is the basis for our word menstruation. Women, the bearers of life, were seen by ancient civilizations as children of the moon goddess. Women can be very powerful, if their deep intuition is blended with spiritual wisdom. The full cycle of Luna must be travelled if wisdom is to be found. This can be achieved easily with meditation and devotion to the heart.

Within the heart of all women is the cycle of love. A woman generally finds it easy to nourish and care for others, to devote her life to beauty and harmony, and to speak from feeling rather than intellect. This reflects her "brightmoon" phase. Then there is the part of a woman that is jealous, possessive, scheming, vengeful, malicious, pre-menstrual – her "darkmoon" phase.

Like women, the moon has cycles. Both of them possess the ability to generate the right conditions for life.

During their menstruation, women find that they are extremely sensitive and highly perceptive. Many ancient civilizations considered them too powerful when they were on their "moontime" and it was common for women to remove themselves from the tribe. Though this is not a practice that is observed in modern societies, it may still be a good idea to set time aside to go within and use each "moontime" as a time to let go of the past cycle, and to allow the flow to cleanse and take away any problems or difficulties, thus making way for the new.

Once wisdom spills into her heart, a woman passes the highest initiation and the lunar cycle takes on its greater perspective. No longer dictated to by emotions, but rather by insight and discrimination, no longer attached, but rhythmical, no longer selfish or jealous but unconditionally compassionate, the wise woman has an extraordinary power.

The Moon and Numerology

In numerology the moon is associated with the number two, a highly feminine number, although in magic she is assigned the number nine. Any years or months that add up to the number two will come under the influence of the moon. Moon years are romantic, creative, unpredictable, deep and intuitive, with a need to bring harmony and stability. However, if the negative aspects of the moon prevail during a number two year, there will be a tendency for depression, cruelty, and possessiveness.

To discover if you are in a moon year, take the four figures and add them together. (For example, the year 2090 becomes 2 + 9 = 11; 1 + 1 = 2.)

Leading up to the present millennium, the year 1999, when broken down into a single number, becomes the number one (1 + 9 + 9 + 9 = 28; 2 + 8 = 10; 1 + 0 = 1). The number one represents the sun.

The year 2000, however, adds up to the number two. Thus, being a lunar year, it heralded an important time to get in touch with inner feelings and emotions, to be with the family, to enhance productivity, and to promote the good of the whole. As the wheel of time turns from sun to moon, so the less predictable but fruitful moon holds sway.

A single halo around a full moon means mild breezes are due.

I	2	3	4	5	6	7	8	9
A	B	C	D	E	F	G	H	I
J	K	L	M	N	O	P	Q	R
S	T	U	V	W	X	Y	Z	

To discover if you are a moon person, take the letters of your chosen name and translate them into numbers using this chart. If they add up to two you will feel a strong affinity with the moon.

Moon people (those whose name or date of birth adds up to the number two) are dedicated parents, have a need for security and emotional reassurance, and have close links with nature and water, in a positive or negative way. Darker aspects of this personality include jealousy, manipulation, deception and vindictiveness. "Two" people need to guard against being two-faced.

Turning Names into Numbers

Using either your full name, your first name or a name that you have chosen for yourself, translate the letters into numbers to discover your affinity with the moon. "Sarah", for example, becomes 2 (1 + 1 + 9 + 1 + 8 = 20; 2 + 0 = 2). Sarahs will therefore feel a strong connection with the attributes of the moon. If you want to work out if you are a moon child, add up the numbers of your full birth date (for example, 2.4.1967 becomes 11 = 1 + 1 = 2).

The Moon and the Weather

The moon has a profound effect upon the earth's climate and atmosphere. She also affects the electromagnetic field that surrounds the earth, creating changes in atmospheric pressure that bring variations in the weather. Research into the moon's effect upon the earth's magnetic field, has shown that the full moon increases the incidents of meteorites falling to earth, and also affects the amount of ozone in the atmosphere.

The earth's magnetic field changes enough, during the monthly cycle of the moon, to affect not only the weather but our health as well, since human beings are sensitive to magnetism. The old wives' tale of feeling things in one's bones can act as a good predictor of rain. Our rheumatic aches and pains can be a valid interpretation of increased dampness in the air.

The moon is known to influence rainfall, to raise storms, tidal flows, earthquakes, hurricanes and volcanic eruptions. Increases in these events have all been recorded just after a full moon. This aspect of the moon's power has psychological effects too. It has been found that mental instability increases dramatically during very unsettled or stormy weather. In severe drought, tribal people would make an offering of precious water to the moon, or milk a cow and offer the fluid in her honour. Clay balls were often flung at the full moon to encourage rain (clay being excellent at retaining water).

The Blue Moon

The old saying "once in a blue moon" refers to a time when two moons occur in the same calendar month, a rather rare occurrence. During the 20th century, for example, there were only 40 blue moons.

A blue moon appears about every two and a half years, usually during a month that has 31 days in it, because there is simply a greater time period in which it can happen. It signifies a special time, a doubling of the moon's powers during the month that she appears. Considered unlucky by some, the blue moon is, in fact, a magical moon, when long-term objectives can be set. So, a blue moon can be used to sow seeds for your future, giving them time to germinate and grow until the next blue moon rises. But you should be careful if you intend to weave magic during a blue moon. Be very clear about what you ask for, because this moon will be potent, doubling your intent.

People born during a blue moon have great potential, but may have difficulty bringing their gifts into action. Their strengths are also their weaknesses, and blue moon people have to learn how to harness their powers to benefit themselves and others.

A blue moon increases the lunar influence on the weather, with a high probability that rainfall, storms and exceptional tides will be more prevalent than usual during that month.

A different type of blue moon occurs when there are certain dust particles in the atmosphere making the moon appear blue.

Because of the power she brings to those born during this time, the blue moon's magic needs to be understood. Those born under a blue moon may have a tendency to moodiness, volatility and emotionalism, as well as the gentler attributes of compassion, caring, sensitivity and natural intuition.

harnessing the moon

harnessing the moon

An appreciation of the rhythms and cycles of the moon can give you new insight into its influence on the world, yourself and those around you, and consequently enhance your understanding of their behaviour. But you can also use this knowledge in more positive ways, grasping the subtle power of the moon to bring benefits into many aspects of your life. The moon's energy is powerful and mysterious, but is always there for you if you are able to tune into its gentle rhythms.

Since it has such a strong influence over the natural patterns of climate and growth you can exploit that strength in your own garden, by planting, sowing and harvesting during the most auspicious lunar phases. There are four phases to be considered. The moon is increasing in influence between the new and full phases (brightmoon) and decreasing in influence between the waning and dark phases (darkmoon).

For your rituals and ceremonies connected with the moon, remember that the moon, like the planets, has particular plants with which she is associated. Flowers of the moon include aquatic plants like water lilies, lotus and watercress, as well as jasmine and poppies. All flowers that are white or that blossom at night come under the regulation of the moon. Arrange a vase of moon flowers on the night of the full or new moon. The willow tree is known as the moon's wishing tree: calling for favour by tying white, silver or light blue ribbons to her branches on lunar festival days can help to draw attention to a wish.

Another moon tree is sandalwood. Associated with protection, purification and healing, chippings of the bark are used in ceremonies requiring these qualities. It has a beautifully calming and soothing smell.

Using plants and flowers of special lunar significance will heighten your sense of connection with the moon. Lunar talismans, used with sensitivity to the moon's cycles, can also help your perception to unfold. The tarot, which includes a depiction of the moon as the Wheel of Fortune, can act as a focus of attention, making a very powerful means of connecting with the intuitive forces of the moon.

Certain crystals have a sympathetic resonance with the cool, subtle energies of the moon. These crystals can help to align your vibrations to hers, inducing clearer dreams, clairvoyant awakening, deeper and truer perceptions and emotional understanding.

All these things can put you in closer touch with the magical mystery of the moon, helping you to foster your intuitive wisdom and balance the rhythm of your life.

lunar gardening
Because the moon has such a strong influence over crop yields, for hundreds of years farmers, agriculturists and gardeners have all used their traditional knowledge of the lunar phases when planting, tending and harvesting crops. This is done by observing the correct phase of the moon for a particular activity, and also by adhering to the sign of the zodiac that it is passing through.

The Cycle

As a general rule, the moon's first and second quarter are the most auspicious times for planting and tending cereal crops, leafy crops and annual plants and flowers. The third quarter is good for root crops and bulbs, trees, shrubs and rhubarb. The fourth quarter is the best time for garden maintenance: for weeding, cultivation and the removal of pests, especially when the moon is in Aries, Gemini, Leo, or Aquarius.

Start a compost heap during the darkmoon time, or harvest and dry herbs and everlasting flowers, especially if the moon is in a fire sign. A water moon is the best time to irrigate fields and gardens.

Each zodiac sign is most auspicious for a particular range of activities in the garden. You will need to consult a lunar calendar to find out when each one falls. However, if to begin with you find it a little too complicated to check the appropriate signs for your gardening tasks, you can simply follow the moon's phases of waxing and waning to reap some of the beneficial effects.

Lunar gardening doesn't mean gardening by night, but rather by the moon's phases through the month.

New Moon

Seeds of plants that flower above the ground should be sown at the new moon. This is the time for farmers to sow cereals such as barley, and for the garden to be planted with asparagus, broccoli, sprouts, cabbage, melons, cauliflower, celery, courgettes, cress, horse-radish, kohlrabi, leeks, peas, peppers, parsley, spinach, squash and tomatoes. This is also the time for fertilizing, feeding and cultivating anything that you wish to flourish and grow.

Full Moon

Around the full moon is the time to plant watery or fleshy plants like marrows and cucumbers. The moon is at her most influential at this time over the water element. This is also a good time for harvesting leaves, stems, or seeds of herbs for drying, especially when the moon is transiting a fire sign. Pick your herbs on a dry day, so that the parts to be harvested will not rot when stored. The best time to harvest is just before midday. String the stems together and hang upside down in an airy but dry atmosphere, until ready for use.

Elemental Gardening Table

Gardening by the moon's phases is very simple once you have mastered the basic principles. Just ensure that you are within the correct moon phase for your gardening task, and that the moon is passing through an appropriate sign. For this, you will need a lunar almanac. Refer to this chart to discover which zodiacal sign is most appropriate for each activity.

AIR	FIRE	WATER	EARTH
Gemini (barren, dry)	**Aries (barren, dry)**	**Cancer (fertile, moist)**	**Taurus (fertile, moist)**
Weeding, clearing, pest control	Weeding, clearing, garden maintenance	Best time for planting, sowing and cultivating	Plant root crops and leafy vegetables
Libra (moist)	**Leo (barren, dry)**	**Scorpio (very fruitful and moist)**	**Virgo (barren, moist)**
Plant fruit trees, fleshy vegetables, root vegetables	Bonfires, ground clearance, weeding	Planting, sowing and general cultivation, especially vines	Cultivation, weeding and pest control
Aquarius (barren, dry)	**Sagittarius (barren, dry)**	**Pisces (fertile, moist)**	**Capricorn (productive, dry)**
Garden maintenance, weeding and pest control	Plant onions, garden maintenance	Excellent for planting, especially root crops	Good for root vegetables

Plant sweetcorn during the new moon to encourage crisp, fleshy kernels of corn.

Farmers should concentrate on cereal crops during the brightmoon phase.

Harvesting your vegetables should be done during a waning or dark moon.

Radishes, carrots and other roots should be planted during a waning moon.

Waning and Dark Moon

The waning moon is the time in the moon's cycle for root vegetables, peas and beans, and garlic. Anything undertaken during this time will benefit underground development or retard growth. This is therefore an excellent time to mow the grass, when its return growth will be slowed, or to plough and turn the soil. Gather and harvest crops during the waning moon, especially in late summer, the traditional harvest time. This is an excellent time to prune trees, roses and shrubs, and to water the garden. Making jams and pickles should also be done during a waning moon, for best results. Establish a compost heap, preferably when the moon is in Scorpio, to increase the fertility of the whole garden.

Crops that are particularly well suited to planting during the waning moon are endive, carrots, garlic, onions, potatoes, radishes, beetroot and strawberries.

All flowering bulbs, biennials, and perennials should be planted during this time, especially when the moon is in a water sign. Saplings also benefit from being planted during the waning moon, when she is in Cancer, Scorpio, Pisces or Virgo.

The principles of lunar gardening take a while to adjust to, but after a while, you will begin to find that your flowers bloom more brightly, your crops grow more succulent and flavoursome and your trees have stronger roots. In fact, your whole garden will benefit from this ancient way of gardening.

A Water Garden Offering to the Moon

The moon goddess Diana's festival days fall upon the May and September full moons each year. At one of these times, you may like to perform a simple water ceremony in your garden or beside a local waterfall, well, stream, lake or river, or possibly on the seashore. The form of this offering is inspired by the ancient art of well-dressing, still practised in some places, when communities "dress" their local source of water with a plaque decorated with symbols, flowers, corn, rice, stones and twigs, placing it by the water as a way of giving thanks.

Perform the ceremony two days before the full moon. As you place your plaque next to the water, you may like to say a prayer to the moon, asking for her blessing and protection for the year to come. Use your own words, as they come.

You will need

- potter's clay
- rolling pin
- knife
- wood, cut to shape
- stick or skewer
- petals, leaves, twigs, shells, flowers, corn, rice, shells and pebbles
- wet cloth

1 Roll out the clay. Use the wooden template and knife to cut the shape from the clay.

2 Press the clay down firmly on to the wood, then mark out your design on the surface.

3 Fill in the design, pushing petals, leaves and other elements into the soft clay.

tarot and the moon

Tarot cards are believed to have originated in Egypt although, like most inherited systems of divination, we cannot be certain of this. In medieval times, the moon was depicted as Fortuna, the Wheel of Fortune in the tarot deck. This card depicts the ups and downs of life, the cycles that represent life's changing fortunes. Like the Wheel of Fortune, the moon is ever-changing, and reminds us that life ebbs and flows.

Reading the Moon Card

The moon card in the tarot deck is numbered 18 (1 + 8). This gives the number nine, which is the magical number of the moon. Nine signifies the completion of a cycle and so signifies a new beginning. Drawing this card tells you that intuition and perception will be your greatest allies in the days to come. Trust your feelings, and take a little time before making decisions of a life-changing nature.

This is a card of feelings and emotions, of all aspects of the feminine, and so may represent an emotional or psychic understanding or change, especially if time is spent in contemplation of the moon's present message.

Number eighteen is the moon card in the tarot deck.

It also conveys a warning that emotionalism and negative reactions that are not tempered with any higher wisdom can lead you into emotional confusion. This card signifies that you are completing one cycle and not yet beginning another – so can raise fears, doubts, and upsets. Don't get carried away with fantasies; stay practical and well grounded in reality, and trust that as every door closes, so another opens.

Take the moon card from the deck and hold it so that the picture is touching your third eye (in the centre of your forehead). Close your eyes and melt into the card, noting symbols, images and feelings that arise.

A Lunar Tarot Card

One way to deepen your connection with the moon is to make your own lunar card. Make up a design of your own that represents the moon for you, just allowing the ideas to form. Make the card just before the new moon, to ensure that your intuition and perception increase as the new moon grows.

You will need

- scissors
- white card
- ruler
- silver pen
- paints or crayons
- paint brush
- glue
- selection of the following: silver glitter, blue and/or silver sequins stars and moon sequin shapes
- pictures of moon animals, birds, trees, crystals, moon flowers, water
- white feathers (dove or duck)
- blue ribbons
- silver tape
- 2 blue or silver candles

1 Cut out a piece of card measuring 9 x 13cm/3½ x 5in and draw your chosen design on it. You can make the card bigger if you feel confident to do so.

2 Paint your design or glue on your chosen collage materials. Let your mind be led by imagination and creativity as you make up your design.

3 If you do not feel confident about drawing a design, cut out pictures of moon animals, trees or flowers, water or crystals and glue them on the card instead. When it is complete, place the card on your altar or special area. Light two blue or silver candles. Meditate upon the images for three nights. Make a note of any unusual dreams you have.

talismans
A talisman can be any small object invested with magical or protective powers, such as a crystal or silver charm. Its potency can be heightened by inscribing it with your sigil, a sign of your name traced on the "kamea", or magic square. In magic, the moon is associated with the number nine. The kamea of the moon adds up to the number nine in all directions and can be used in magic to connect with the powers and gifts the moon provides.

Attracting and Releasing Talismans

When you are making a lunar talisman it is important to observe the correct timing: from the new moon to the full moon is the time for drawing things to you, and from the full moon to the beginning of the dark moon is the time for releasing things. For example, if you are seeking new beginnings or fertility, use the new moon, and if you are asking for healing, use the waning time. The new to full phase is for growth and attraction. The waning to dark phase is for decrease and removal.

Place an attracting talisman in the light of the moon with a moonstone or white circular stone on top, until your wish is granted. Take a releasing talisman to a river or seashore on the first night after a full moon and place it in the water to be taken away. Watch it leave, and then turn away. Do not look back.

To make your talisman you will first need to work out the sigil of your name. Convert your name into numerals using the numerology chart. For example, "Isabel" becomes the numbers 911253. Trace the shape those numbers make on the kamea. Begin with a small circle, then draw a line connecting the numerals until you have a sigil, or pattern. Isabel would begin by joining nine to one, then one to two and so on. End the sigil with a line.

The sigil of Isabel makes this pattern on the kamea.

The Kamea of the Moon
A lunar kamea can be used to balance the emotions, to call for fertility, and to enhance perceptions and psychic abilities, as well as for journeys at night or over water.

37	78	29	70	21	62	13	54	5
6	38	79	30	71	22	63	14	46
47	7	39	80	31	72	23	55	15
16	48	8	40	81	32	64	24	56
57	17	48	9	41	73	33	65	25
26	58	18	50	1	42	74	34	66
67	27	59	10	51	2	43	75	35
36	68	19	60	11	52	3	44	76
77	28	69	20	61	12	53	4	45

A Lunar Talisman

Use the sigil of your name to make an attracting talisman on which you can write a wish, and then leave it in the moonlight until your wish is granted.

You will need

- 2 silver or white candles
- matches
- silver pen
- ruler
- 23cm/9in square of natural paper

I Light two silver or white candles, invoking the aid of the moon as you do so with these words: *"Hail to you, Levanah. I light these candles in your honour and ask for your assistance this night."*

2 Draw a 5cm/2in square in the top left-hand corner of a square sheet of natural paper. Copy the sigil of your name (do not include any numbers from the kamea with it) into the square using a silver pen.

3 Write your wish (this might be for a safe journey, for example) in the remaining space on the paper. Fold the four corners of the paper into the centre to make a diamond shape, then repeat the folds twice more.

4 Leave your talisman on a windowsill or somewhere in the light of the moon, to draw her favour to your wish. Place a moonstone, or some other circular white stone to represent the moon, on top of the folded talisman.

lunar crystals, colours and circles

The moon has been associated with particular sacred stones for thousands of years. Traditionally, white, clear or watery bright stones are associated with the waxing and full moon and black or dark stones with the waning and dark aspects when insights can be gained and wisdom can be sought. They will help to align your vibrations with those of the moon.

Bright Moontime Crystals

You can take your crystals to lakes or the seashore during a full moon and cleanse them there in the water.

Celestite, in its blue or white varieties, links you to your spirit guides, to light your way in the dreamtime.

Azurite, known as the stone of Heaven, can help you attune your mind to the psychic world.

Pearls are symbolic of the moon because they come from the sea and represent purity, clarity and grace.

Aquamarine makes an ideal dream crystal, tuning you into the rhythms of the sea and into the depths of your own spirit.

Circular white stones or pebbles of any kind can be used to represent the full moon, or to increase your connections with her.

Clear quartz looks like frozen water, and has a strong affinity with the moon. It can be used in healing or invoking ceremonies.

Moonstone can be used to balance the hormonal cycle, calm any unsettled emotions, and help induce lucid dreaming.

Dark Moontime Crystals

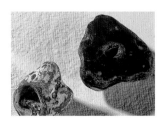

Holy flint is normal flint but with a natural hole in it. It can protect the wearer from night terrors, fears and from negative thought forms.

Jet, a deeply black mineral, is symbolic of the dark moon. It clears a heavy head, and can help in the lifting of depression or gloominess.

Black stones can be found by the riverside or on beach walks. Carry them with you whenever you are feeling confused or disorientated.

Citrine is actually a crystal of the sun. It has been included here as a preventer of nightmares, to enable you to get a good night's sleep.

Casting a Brightmoon Circle

This ceremony can be performed every month to honour the moon, as the protector and guardian of women. When women cast the circle it will refresh and rejuvenate them for the month to come. For a man it will have a symbolic rather than biological significance as he follows his own rhythms and cycles from the female within. The ceremony can be done indoors or outdoors, during the two days leading up to a full moon.

As you light the candles, say: "Magna Dei, light of the night, I light these candles to guide your moonrays here. I ask you to come and bless this circle." Once you are standing in the circle, say the lunar invocation: "Hail to thee, Sophia, holy spirit of the wise moon. I call upon you to enter and fill me with your light. Protect me and guide me on the moonway. Teach me your wisdom and truth as I seek your clarity and guidance."

Imagine yourself drawing down the powers of the moon into yourself. Allow yourself to be refreshed and re-filled with the feminine virtues of wisdom, beauty and grace. Let the moon bless your feelings and perceptions until you feel energized and content. Bring your arms down to your sides. Close your circle by saying "Thank you". Blow out your candles and dispose of organic ingredients outside.

You will need

- 13 circular stones, river stones or moon crystals
- salt
- aromatherapy burner
- matches
- jasmine essential oil
- 9 candles

1 Turning clockwise, lay down 12 of your chosen stones (these can be all different sizes) in a circle around you, beginning in the south. Place the last stone in the centre.

2 Sprinkle each of the stones around the circle with a little salt. Light the aromatherapy burner and put in three drops of jasmine essential oil.

3 Place eight candles around the circle and one by the centre stone. As you light the candles, say the invocation to Mother Moon.

4 Facing south, stand with your arms outstretched above your head and your feet quite wide apart. Reach towards the sky.

Lunar Colours

The moon has colours that are traditionally associated with her. Use and wear them when you are performing ceremonies, or simply to maintain your connection with the moon's phases.

White, associated with purity and innocence, represents the new moon. White and milky stones are also associated with the new moon. Burn white candles when working during this phase – for example, to call for new opportunities. Silver has the most favourable lunar associations, because of its coolness and fluidity. Silver jewellery, especially when worn during the new to full moon phase, can enhance all the magical qualities of the moon.

Light blue is a very healing colour. It can soothe, calm and cool heated emotions, illness, or burns and stings. Once appropriate medical attention has been administered, visualize a light blue colour bathing a specific area, or the whole person, and you will notice a marked reduction in the symptoms.

Black is the colour of the darkmoon, when the inner world can speak most clearly. It is associated with Hecate, goddess of death and the underworld. Black is a silent, inward colour, so can be worn as protection or when seeking insight. It is a colour of power and identity. Burn white candles during the darkmoon phase, and meditate in black clothes or cloaked in a black cloth.

If you feel drawn to setting up an altar to the full moon, you may like to use a light blue cloth, silver candles, sandalwood incense and wild water meadow or riverside flowers.

astrology

astrology astrology

As long ago as 30,000 BC early humans were charting the passage of the stars across the night sky. We know this from finds of bone fragments that have definite star cycles marked on them. But it was the Chaldeans from Assyria who first recorded that the stars ran in a fixed way but that planets wandered. They could see that these wanderers – the Moon, Venus, Mercury, Mars, Jupiter and Saturn – passed in front of fixed star positions, which they called constellations, and that the affairs and events of humans seemed to be linked with the passage of these planets. As each planet moved into and through the backdrop of a particular constellation, similar events seemed to occur. For instance, when Mars was visible humans seemed more ready to go to battle – hence Mars was called the god of war. Venus, on the other hand, seemed to promote peace and harmony, and was called the goddess of love. Thus was formed the basis of astrology around the seventh century BC.

Gradually, the movements of the stars and planets were observed over longer periods of time, and the more subtle relationships between their positions on the horizons and human nature were verified, and astrology came to be part of everyday life. It became clear that the power of foresight or divination could be used to advantage to improve and predict relationships between subjects and rulers, countries and kingdoms. Astrology was to stay, for all time.

the sun signs
Your sun sign dominates everything else. It is the outer you, the part you show to others, and it is difficult to hide. Your sun sign is the one you read about in daily horoscopes in newspapers and magazines, and these analyses are based on twelve possible birth periods. You may share characteristics of the sign next to yours if you were born within a few days of the next or previous sign – this is known as being on the cusp.

Aries 22 March–20 April ♈
The Aries character is one of adventure and enterprise. If you are a typical Aries you will know no fear. You have extremely high energy levels, love your freedom and hate having any sort of discipline imposed on you. You can be quick-tempered and impulsive. You may well be impatient – you want everything now. You are, however, enthusiastic and generous and very quick-thinking in emergencies.

Taurus 21 April–21 May ♉
The Taurus character is one of reliability, strength and patience. If you are a typical Taurus you will have limitless energy to see through any project you start. You are stubborn and relentless but have a broad back to cope with life's adversities. You are a lover of good food and wines and work hard for luxury. You have a very strong moral code and stick to strict high principles in everything you do.

Gemini 22 May–22 June ♊
The Gemini character is entertaining, lively and a good communicator. A typical Gemini is quick-witted, highly intelligent and extremely versatile – there is nothing a true Gemini won't try to turn their hand to. You have strong opinions but may change them. You can be extremely amusing and talkative and have a great flair for languages and ideas. Gemini is known as the Two Stars – Castor and Pollux (or Hercules and Apollo) represent its communicating aspect – you always need (and have) someone to talk to.

Cancer 23 June–23 July ♋
The Cancer character is caring and protective. A typical Cancer will feel things deeply and care a great deal about loved ones. You can be over-emotional and too sensitive sometimes but you are sympathetic and kind. You have very strong intuition and imagination. You have strong parenting instincts and depths of feelings which others can only guess at. Cancer is represented in the constellations as the Crab – you need desperately to be by water but you also need the land to give you your reality.

Leo 24 July–23 August ♌
The Leo character is dominant and powerful, and won't shun the limelight. You are creative, enthusiastic and energetic. You can be too dramatic but you have talents, charm and personality. You are a great organizer and love being surrounded by people and action. The Sun is represented by the lion killed by Hercules and the lion's mane is Leo's distinguishing feature – your hair is important to you.

Virgo 24 August–23 September ♍
The Virgo character has good taste and refinement; a typical Virgo won't put up with anything that is only second-best. You are tidy and organized and expect as much of others. You have strict rules and could be seen as fussy or critical. However, you are meticulous, work hard and delight in constant activity. The Virgo character's namesake was the goddess of justice.

Libra 24 September–23 October ♎
The Libra character is calm and rational. A typical Libra will be charming, loved and respected. You like an easy-going life and are idealistic and romantic. You may be seen as frivolous because you back away from confrontation and unpleasantness but you are refined and elegant and don't need confusion around you. Libra is represented by the Scales – you see balance in everything and weigh all decisions carefully. You understand give and take and are prepared to compromise – sometimes too readily.

Scorpio 24 October–22 November ♏
The Scorpio character is one of indulgence and excess, passion and emotions. If you are a typical Scorpio you will feel things intensely and be driven by a strong sense of purpose. You are discerning and imaginative. Whatever you dedicate yourself to you will do wholeheartedly and completely. You have great endurance and strength and are a powerful person. Scorpio is represented by the scorpion who rose from the earth to attack Orion. You have a hard outer shell but are warm and soft inside – however, you are the one with the sting in your tail.

Sagittarius 23 November–22 December

The Sagittarius character is one of freedom, loving travel and a search for knowledge and depth in all things. If you are a typical Sagittarius you simply love to know. You keep an open mind and are adaptable and friendly. You are wise and clever with sound judgement and a responsible nature. You value your freedom highly and do not like discipline, rules or routine. You are a seeker after truth and knowledge above all things. Sagittarius is represented by the centaur Chiron: half-man, half-horse, to symbolize your love of travelling, with a drawn bow to symbolize your ability to cut straight to the truth.

Capricorn 23 December–19 January

The Capricorn character may be seen as very serious but in reality you are determined and relentless. If you are a typical Capricorn you place great emphasis on hard work, fulfilling your obligations and improving. You don't like to stand still and be bored. You are a determined seeker after understanding and power. You are ambitious and persevering. You have a tremendous sense of humour and fun but don't allow it to show except when you are with very close friends. The world sees you as steady and reliable. Capricorn is symbolized by Pan, the goat, a seducer of nymphs and a knower of secret things.

Aquarius 20 January–19 February

The Aquarius character is one of independence and friendliness. There is nothing you wouldn't do for others. If you are a typical Aquarius you will be modern in your outlook. You follow your ruling planet closely – you collect nothing and get rid of everything. You prune everything in your life – friendships, ideals, dreams and goals – closely and carefully. You are interested in ideas not possessions. You are an intellectual, and are inventive and resourceful. You are a loyal idealist, kind and a champion of the underdog. Aquarius is symbolized by the upturned water jug – a constant stream of ideas and inspiration.

Pisces 20 February–21 March

The Pisces character is one of change and intuition. If you are a typical Pisces you change your feelings many times during a day and you feel everything intensely. You are kind and receptive and genuinely care about others. Like any water – changing from ice to water, from water to steam, and back to water – the true Pisces character cannot be grasped, for it is unworldly and nebulous. Pisces is symbolized by Venus and Cupid, who changed themselves into fish to escape the amorous advances of the giant Typhon.

Sun Sign Qualities

Each of the 12 sun signs has a masculine or feminine quality, as well as an element – fire, water, earth or air – which governs it. Each sign also has a general quality: it is either cardinal (that is, it initiates things), mutable (it sees things through) or fixed (it completes things). Each sign has a ruling planet which gives it its strengths and qualities.

Aries is the first sign of the zodiac and its ruling planet is Mars, the god of war. Aries is a cardinal masculine fire sign. Keywords for Aries are urgent and assertive.

Taurus is the second sign of the zodiac and its ruling planet is Venus, goddess of love. Taurus is a fixed feminine earth sign. Keywords for Taurus are determined and honourable.

Gemini is the third sign of the zodiac and its ruling planet is Mercury, the messenger. Gemini is a mutable masculine air sign. Keywords for Gemini are versatile and expressive.

Cancer is the fourth sign of the zodiac and its ruling planet is the Moon, goddess of the emotions. Cancer is a cardinal feminine water sign. Keywords for Cancer are intuitive and emotional.

Leo is the fifth sign of the zodiac and its ruling planet is the Sun, king of the universe. Leo is a fixed masculine fire sign. Keywords for Leo are powerful and dramatic.

Virgo is the sixth sign of the zodiac and its ruling planet is Mercury, the messenger. Virgo is a mutable feminine earth sign. Keywords for Virgo are discriminating and analytical.

Libra is the seventh sign of the zodiac and its ruling planet is Venus, goddess of love. Libra is a cardinal masculine air sign. Keywords for Libra are harmony and diplomacy.

Scorpio is the eighth sign of the zodiac and its ruling planet is Pluto, planet of regeneration and change. Scorpio is a fixed feminine water sign. Keywords for Scorpio are passion and power.

Sagittarius is the ninth sign of the zodiac and its ruling planet is Jupiter, planet of wisdom and vision. Sagittarius is a mutable masculine fire sign. Keywords for Sagittarius are freedom and optimism.

Capricorn is the tenth sign of the zodiac and its ruling planet is Saturn, planet of practicality and lessons to be learnt. Capricorn is a cardinal feminine earth sign. Keywords for Capricorn are duty and discipline.

Aquarius is the eleventh sign of the zodiac and its ruling planet is Uranus, planet of elimination. Aquarius is a fixed masculine air sign. Keywords for Aquarius are independence and compassion.

Pisces is the twelfth and last sign of the zodiac and is ruled by the planet Neptune, watery god of the depths. Pisces is a mutable feminine water sign. Keywords for Pisces are nebulous and receptive.

the houses

The sky is divided into twelve sectors, each known as a house. The houses are not heavenly bodies or star systems but they neatly cover every area of human development. The house in which a planet or a constellation lies is important as it gives a clue to the area that will be influenced. The planet shows how something will manifest, the constellation gives the manner of its manifestation and the house indicates what it will affect.

The 12th house represents what we fear and cannot know: unconscious impulses, seclusion, sleep and death.

First House: Birth
The first house represents your basic personality, physical health, the way you reveal yourself to others around you and your physical appearance.

Second House: Possessions
The second house represents what you own. It is bound up with wealth, material possessions and personal belongings. It also represents feeling.

Third House: the Mind
The third house is to do with how you think about the world, communicate ideas and how you express yourself.

Fourth House: the Home
The fourth house is about where you live: your roots, your ancestry, your parents and family.

Fifth House: Creativity
This is the house of pleasure, leisure and socializing.

Sixth House: Work
The house of employment, business, career opportunities and working relationships.

Seventh House: the Heart
The seventh is the house of relationships and love affairs, marriage and long-term partnerships.

Eighth House: Sharing
The eighth is the house of attitudes, whether on sex, money or ideas. It is where you reveal your generosity – or lack thereof.

Ninth House: the Intellect
The ninth house represents how you learn: your education and upbringing but also your study as an adult in later life.

Tenth House: Personal Ambitions
This is the house of your aspirations: your dreams and goals, longings and drives.

11th house: Friendship
The 11th house is to do with how you entertain your friends and social acquaintances, and with the way you indulge your personal pleasures.

12th House: Escapism
The 12th is the house of seclusion and loneliness, death and the unconscious. It represents what you fear.

The 10th house covers the area of your worldly ambitions, aspirations and drive to success in your life.

the planets

Although strictly speaking the sun is not a planet but a star, it is still included as a planet in charts for astrological purposes. In terms of the zodiac, everything revolves around the earth, which lies at the very centre of your chart. As the exploration of space progresses and we begin to travel to other planets, it may be that astrologers will need to draw up new charts, with earth as one of the planets and perhaps Mars or Venus in the centre.

The Sun
This is the most important of the planets. It governs character and determines power and vitality, life and growth.

The Moon
For insights into your emotional side, the moon is the place to look. It is mysterious and dark, deep and secret. It is the planet of the imagination.

Mercury
The planet of communication is Mercury the messenger. It governs the way in which you express yourself and communicate with others. It is also the planet that rules the area of mental powers.

Venus
The planet of love is Venus. It is also the planet of beauty and the appreciation of fine things. It is refined and harmonious.

Mars
The planet of war, Mars, is the planet of conflict and disagreements. It represents aggression and force, power and dynamic movement. It is also the planet of sex.

Saturn is the planet of practicality and lessons to be learnt. It is the ruler of the sun sign Capricorn.

Jupiter
The planet of Jupiter is luck and kindness. It governs pleasure and recreation. Jupiter is a planet of philosophy and expansion.

Saturn
This is the planet of lessons. It tells you what it is that you need to learn in order to progress or move on. It is the planet of duty and responsibility, security and discipline.

Uranus
This planet represents what you need to eliminate from your life, and what you need to avoid repeating. It is the planet of change and sudden unexpected events.

Neptune
The planet of religion and spirituality is Neptune. It is here you should look for your intuition and imagination. Neptune represents the realm of idealism and sensitivity.

Pluto
The planet of the 12th House: Pluto – the unconscious. It governs the way you think and feel about death, and the dark secret things you fear most.

Venus is the planet of love and beauty, personified by the goddess of love. It rules the feminine signs Taurus and Libra.

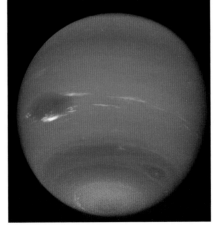

Neptune is the planet of spirituality, personified by the ruler of the sea. It rules the water sign Pisces.

Mars is the fiery planet of conflict, personified by the god of war. It rules the masculine fire sign Aries.

using astrology

Once the foundations of astrology had been laid, a way was devised to represent the heavens on paper so the positions of all the planets, stars, constellations and houses could be plotted. A circular representation was used with the earth in the centre surrounded by the heavens. The sun was regarded as a planet – although supremely important – and was depicted as revolving around the earth with the rest of the planets.

The Zodiac

The circular chart of the heavens was called a zodiac – which, in old French and Greek, means circle of animal signs – as an animal was chosen to represent each constellation of stars. Originally a zodiac was drawn up only to forecast the outcome of major events and catastrophes, such as a forthcoming war, a flood or a plague. Gradually, as events seemed to be linked to a country's ruler, a zodiac chart would be drawn up for the king of the people. This was taken very seriously in China where the succession was determined astrologically: as each child was born to the ruling emperor, a court astrologer would see whether the auspices were right for them to become the heir to the throne. The notion of a personal chart gradually spread from the ruler to his subjects.

In this celestial chart, the constellations are shown as animals circling the earth.

based on the observations of countless millions of people. The only test of astrology is to try it for yourself and see how accurate it is for you.

Astrology cannot foretell the future, but it can illuminate the basic building blocks of your personality, character and potential, for you to make what you will of them. The gravitational and electromagnetic effects of the moon are well known, so what effect may the pull of the planets, the electromagnetic influences of the stars and solar activity have on us? We know the sun can influence radio reception on earth in quite dramatic ways and, despite our sophistication, we are very sensitive creatures. There may be a more scientific basis to astrology than we have yet been able to discover.

Your Personal Chart

As a visual reference to your life the zodiac chart is both mathematically intricate and beautifully simple. It shows the exact moment in the history of the universe at which you entered it, and thus begins your own personal history. Your chart could only be identical to someone else's if they were born at the same moment as you and in exactly the same place.

The zodiac still shows the earth at the centre and has the 12 constellations, the 12 houses and the planets surrounding it. The additional planets Uranus, Neptune and Pluto were included as they were discovered, and are known as the fixed planets as they move so slowly that they influence a whole generation.

The position of the planets in relation to one another on your birth chart is known as the aspect. Aspects are major or minor depending on their angle relative to one another. This angle determines how they affect you.

How Astrology Works

Astrology is based on the expected turn of events. Around 9,000 years of observations have shown that when planets are in certain positions, some things are much more likely to occur. However, nothing is set in stone, and nothing will guarantee that events will turn out in a particular way, but the probabilities are

Finding your Sign

Each sign is represented by an animal or mythical character which symbolizes its inherent nature. Your sun sign shows which constellation was behind the sun at your birth. While this cannot give as much information as an entire chart, it can help you to understand yourself in astrological terms. To have a chart prepared for you, you will need to visit an astrologer or find a computer programme that will do it for you.

Sun Sign Dates

Aries: 22 March – 20 April

Taurus: 21 April – 21 May

Gemini: 22 May – 22 June

Cancer: 23 June – 23 July

Leo: 24 July – 23 August

Virgo: 24 August – 23 September

Libra: 24 September – 23 October

Scorpio: 24 October – 22 November

Sagittarius: 23 November – 22 December

Capricorn: 23 December – 19 January

Aquarius: 20 January – 19 February

Pisces: 20 February – 21 March

astrology and you

An astrological chart will show how you are likely to react in love or business, how your basic personality might appear to those around you – and those things that you like to keep secret. And of course this applies equally to other people close to you. What better way can there be to know how your lover or business might respond to a situation than to look at their astrological chart?

Personality

Your character is revealed by your sun sign and is the fundamental you. Your personality, however, is how you come across to other people and is revealed by your ascendant or rising sign: the constellation on the eastern horizon at the time of your birth. For instance, Aries is a dynamic sign with leadership qualities and a forthright approach to life, but an ascendant in Cancer might make those qualities somewhat muted and kinder. On the other hand, an Aries with a Scorpio ascendant would lead in a much more rigid and authoritarian manner. An Aries with a Sagittarius ascendant might be happier leading only very small groups.

The typical Aries character is fearless and adventurous.

There are 12 signs and 12 ascendants, giving 144 possible combinations. You may find it is simply not enough to say "I am a Taurean" or "I am a Capricorn". It becomes increasingly necessary to add to that definition, and say "I'm a Taurean with Virgo rising" or "I'm Capricorn with Pisces rising".

Character

Your sun sign is the real you, but it is modified by your rising sign, and by the position of the moon and the mid-heaven in your chart. This gives four distinct parts to your character and 20,736 possible combinations, without looking at other factors in your chart such as the position of the planets, houses or aspects. Astrologers are usually pretty good at "guessing" your sun sign: actually they aren't guessing at all but reading the clues you yourself present to them.

Relationships

The moon governs your emotional side whereas the sun rules your outer personality. Your moon is the secret, loving part of you that you keep hidden except in a trusting and loving relationship. You need to check which constellation and which house it appears. Next to the sun, the moon sign is the most important part of your chart and not only shows your emotional side but also your relationships with your family, your parents and your children, as well as your dreams, goals and aspirations.

The moon rules Cancer, which is the sign of home, security and protection. The nearer to Cancer the moon appears in your chart, the closer you will be to these qualities. Compare your moon with your lover's to see how compatible you are. If your two moons are in opposition you can expect clashes, whereas if they are in conjunction (next to each other) then you will be helpful and loving to each other.

Career

Your mid-heaven, at the top of your chart, tells you which constellation was directly overhead when you were born and points to career possibilities. If your mid-heaven falls in Aries, you will be dynamic at work, a leader and in charge. A Taurean mid-heaven would ideally be suited to farming or horticulture. Gemini points to a career as an entrepreneur or sales person. Cancer indicates work in a caring profession such as counselling or therapy. Leo would indicate someone in the public eye, such as an actor or politician. Virgo would be happiest working in research, planning or computer programming. Libra would be ideally suited to design work. Scorpio is best suited to anything secret, such as spying, research or crime writing. Sagittarius is the traveller of the career world. Capricorn is best at anything that requires an organized, methodical approach. Aquarius is best involved with new ideas – science, analysis, and inventing. Pisces is the problem-solver of the zodiac, best in advertising, charity work or astrology.

Geminis have strong opinions, and are good communicators.

compatibility chart

This chart is designed to show which signs are compatible in love, but don't dismiss incompatible signs altogether – you may be suited in other ways. While a romantic pairing looks inauspicious, a different kind of relationship might be successful. For instance, Aries people can never seem to fall in love with Taureans, but they certainly can go into business with them and are likely to do very well indeed.

	Aries ♈	Taurus ♉	Gemini ♊	Cancer ♋	Leo ♌	Virgo ♍	Libra ♎	Scorpio ♏	Sagittarius ♐	Capricorn ♑	Aquarius ♒	Pisces ♓
Aries ♈	✓	✓✓	✓	✓✓	✓✓✓	✓✓	XXX	XX	✓✓✓	XX	✓✓	✓✓
Taurus ♉	✓✓	✓	XX	✓✓	XX	✓✓✓	XX	XXX	✓	✓✓✓	XX	✓
Gemini ♊	✓	XX	✓	✓✓	✓✓	XX	✓✓✓	✓	XXX	XX	✓✓✓	✓✓
Cancer ♋	✓✓	✓✓	✓✓	✓	XX	✓✓	XX	✓✓	XX	XXX	✓✓	✓✓✓
Leo ♌	✓✓✓	XX	✓✓	XX	XX	✓✓	✓	XX	✓✓✓	✓	XXX	✓✓
Virgo ♍	✓✓	✓✓✓	XX	✓✓	✓✓	✓	XX	✓✓	XX	✓✓✓	✓	XXX
Libra ♎	XXX	XX	✓✓✓	XX	✓	XX	✓	✓✓	XX	✓✓	✓✓✓	✓
Scorpio ♏	XX	XXX	✓	✓✓	XX	✓✓	✓✓	✓✓	✓✓	XX	✓	✓✓✓
Sagittarius ♐	✓✓✓	✓	XXX	XX	✓✓✓	XX	XX	✓✓	✓✓	✓	✓✓	✓✓
Capricorn ♑	XX	✓✓✓	XX	XXX	✓	✓✓✓	✓✓	XX	✓	XX	XX	✓✓
Aquarius ♒	✓✓	XX	✓✓✓	✓✓	XXX	✓	✓✓	✓	✓✓	XX	✓✓	✓✓
Pisces ♓	✓✓	✓	✓✓	✓✓✓	✓✓	XXX	✓	✓✓✓	✓✓	✓✓	✓✓	XX

Key to Symbols

✓ These two signs are not particularly compatible but will have no real problems. They will probably simply ignore each other.

✓✓ This combination is not bad at all. Two people with these signs will get along fine and are likely to become very close.

✓✓✓ Very compatible. Lovers for life – good business partners – good marriage partners – good friends.

XX Bad move. These two signs are not at all compatible in a relationship. These two will certainly not like each other much.

XXX Sparks will fly. These two positively dislike each other – they won't even stay in the same room. They will be deadly enemies.

birth chart

A natal chart is drawn up for the moment a person is born. An astrologer would need your birth date and the exact time and place for accuracy. The chart below was compiled for Alex, who was born in the United States on 17th June 1943. Alex is an entertainer who travels the world. He was brought up by his father after his parents divorced. He has never married and enjoys a large income. He lives alone but has a global audience.

Reading the Chart

The inner circle, marked 1–12, indicates the positions of the houses. Within it, aspect lines link up any planetary positions that are of interest, such as oppositions, conjunctions, trines (120° angles) and squares (90° angles). The middle ring shows the planets and the outer ring gives the positions of the constellations at the time of Alex's birth.

To the right of the chart, the first table shows what the symbols mean. The second shows in which constellation and in which house each planet is to be found. The third table explains where the houses fall. You can see that the ascendant is in the first house, the descendant in the seventh and the mid-heaven in the tenth.

At the top are listed Alex's name and date of birth; the house system that is being used (in this case the equal system); the time zone he was born in; which aspects are being shown (in this case, "strong orbs" means that only the most dominant aspects, such as oppositions, conjunctions, trines and squares, have been plotted); and the longitude and latitude of his place of birth.

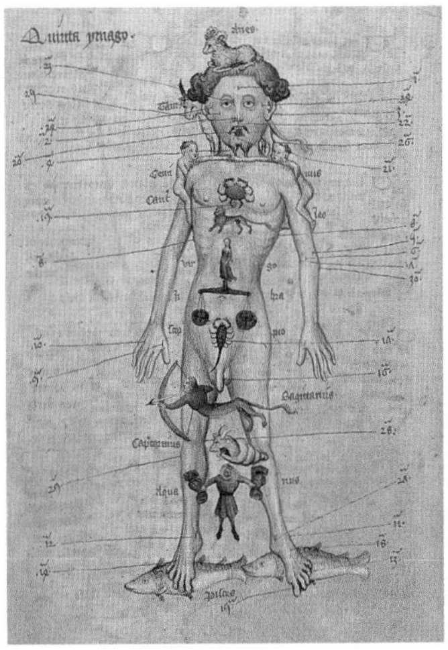

It was always considered that each astrological sign ruled a particular part of the body.

Interpreting the Chart

An astrologer could gain a considerable amount of information from this chart. For instance Alex's Sun is in Gemini in the 11th house. This would give him a very visible public image, with clear objectives and great personal success – someone who brings happiness to others by their personality, charisma and ability to entertain.

Alex has his Sun and Moon in opposition: this means he is a person in whom the sun is a very powerful focus; someone who will have extreme tendencies, which may be theatrical or political; it can also indicate problems between his parents.

His mid-heaven (career) is in Taurus which indicates someone who is comfortable, successful and would do well in farming or the arts. His ascendant (rising sign) is in Leo, which again indicates someone who enjoys the spotlight and will be in the public eye. His Moon is in Sagittarius in the fourth house – this shows someone who won't settle into a relationship easily but enjoys travel a lot, and likes their own company but still needs a very comfortable luxurious home base to return to.

Alex	**Thursday**	**Equal**	**Strong Orbs**
	17/06/43 09:00:00	**Time Zone:5:00W**	**Summer Time: 0:00**
			40N38 73W56

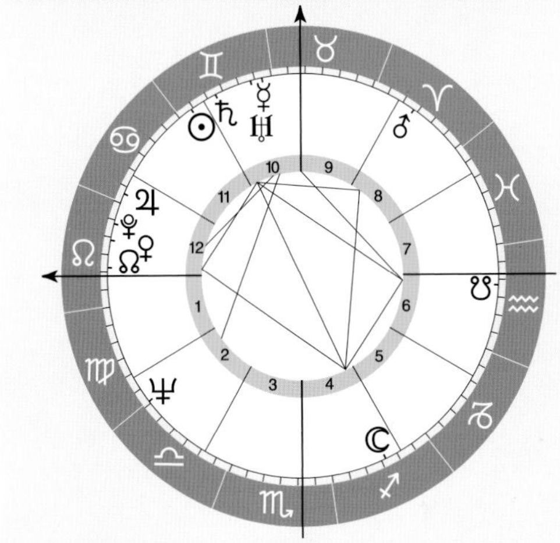

Planetary symbols		Constellation symbols		Planetary position with houses				House position		
☉	Sun	♈	Aries	☉	25.30	♊	11	Asc	21.21	♌
☽	Moon	♉	Taurus	☽	16.40	♐	4	2	21.21	♍
☿	Mercury	♊	Gemini	☿	2.46	♊	10	3	21.21	♎
♀	Venus	♋	Cancer	♀	10.32	♌	12	Ic	21.21	♏
♂	Mars	♌	Leo	♂	15.32	♈	8	5	21.21	♐
♃	Jupiter	♍	Virgo	♃	27.13	♋	12	6	21.21	♑
♄	Saturn	♎	Libra	♄	17.17	♊	10	Dsc	21.21	♒
♅	Uranus	♏	Scorpio	♅	5.54	♊	10	8	21.21	♓
♆	Neptune	♐	Sagittarius	♆	29.17	♍	2	9	21.21	♈
♇	Pluto	♑	Capricorn	♇	5.40	♌	12	Msc	21.21	♉
☊	N.Node	♒	Aquarius	☊	18.38	♌	12	11	21.21	♊
☋	S.Node	♓	Pisces	☋	18.38	♒	6	12	21.21	♋

chinese astrology
chinese astrology

chinese astrology

According to legend, when the Buddha found enlightenment under a fig tree he invited all the animals in creation to share in his joy. Only 12 accepted, however, and it is these who are honoured by being included in the Chinese zodiac. Each animal was allotted its own year to govern.

Chinese astrology is very old. Although the Buddha lived two and a half millennia ago (563–483 BC), the truth is that no one actually knows how old it is and it may well predate him. There are some who date its origin as far back as the reign of the legendary Yellow Emperor of China, who lived around 2630 BC. What we do know is that the system, still in wide use today in China and other eastern countries, has remained unchanged for several thousand years. Until even quite recently, it would have been unthinkable for anyone in these countries to have married, moved house, changed jobs, conceived a child or even celebrated a happy event without first getting advice from an astrologer.

Astrological studies reached their peak in China during the Han dynasty (200 BC–AD 200), but at one time, the Emperor banned "ordinary" people from using astrology at all on the grounds that it was dangerous. He considered the information it imparted so accurate that it could be used to plot against him and his court. So he simply banned its use – except for himself, naturally.

the philosophy of chinese astrology

Chinese astrology was influenced by Taoism, one of the ancient religions of China. The Tao (the Way) says that everything in the universe has a quality or aspect which is either male or female, advancing or retiring, light or dark. Everything is in a state of constant change between the two opposites, which are not in conflict with each other but are complementary.

Yin and Yang

The opposites are called yang (male) and yin (female) and they are represented by a symbol in which each half contains a tiny seed of the opposite aspect, indicating their interdependence. Both qualities are essential and balance each other: together they make us complete.

The Five Elements

The basic qualities are further defined by one of the five elements – water, wood, fire, metal or earth. Each animal and each year is either yin or yang and is governed by an element. The animals are divided into four groups: water – rat, ox and pig; wood – tiger, hare and dragon; fire – snake, horse and goat; metal – monkey, rooster and dog. Earth rules no animals but it lends its qualities to some of the years.

The yin-yang symbol.

The Sixty-year Cycle

As there are 12 animals and five elements in the Chinese astrological system, they give rise to 60 different animal types, succeeding one another in rotation through a 60-year cycle, with half of the years being yin and half being yang. This 60-year cycle is important as it makes each year special and unique – you are not just a particular animal (one of 12) but a particular type of animal. If you happen to be a yang water tiger, for example, your character and life will be very different from that of a yang wood tiger. If you then add in the 12 months of the year, which also affect Chinese horoscopes, and the 12 divisions for the times of day, you can see that this gives a total of 8640 possible combinations of horoscopes (five elements × 12 animals × 12 months × 12 times of day).

Clockwise from top

Water is associated with the north: communication, sensitivity and intuition.

Wood is associated with the east: nurturing, creativity and growth.

Fire is associated with the south: passion, intelligence and movement.

Metal is associated with the west: useful and dependable.

Earth is the centre: balance, reliability, foundations.

using chinese astrology In addition to lending its

characteristics to people born during a particular year, each animal also influences the quality of the year itself. So knowing which animal rules a future year can help you to plan for the trials and triumphs that year might bring. For instance, dragons are usually associated with expansion and prosperity, so a dragon year might be an auspicious time to start a new business.

Inner and Secret Animals

You have more than one animal sign which governs your life, and it is important that you work out your inner and secret animals too. Your inner animal is worked out by the month in which you were born – the lunar month. This controls your love life, so if you want to find out whether you are compatible with another sign, you need to know both your own inner animal and your potential partner's. Your secret animal is determined by the time of your birth, and it is this animal which will reveal the true you – to yourself only of course. So if you were born at 08.00 in February 1963, outwardly you are a hare, your inner animal is the tiger, and your secret animal is the dragon.

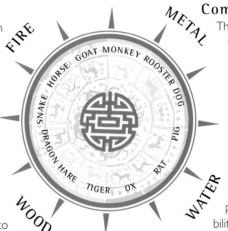

Use this chart to check your compatibility.

Compatibility

This information helps you to find out what each year (and each month) could bring you, and it can also be informative when you are thinking about the people around you. Suppose you are considering going into business with a friend, for instance. You can find out what animal he or she is, and you know what sort of animal you are – so are the two compatible? Would a pig make a good business partner for a rat? Look at the compatibility chart on the left for a quick at-a-glance check, and use the same information for personal relationships; are you compatible with your lover? You can even use the chart to look at friendships: the compatibilities don't change.

Animal Months and Hours

Rat: December, 11pm – 1am

Ox: January, 1am – 3am

Tiger: February, 3am – 5am

Hare: March, 5am – 7am

Dragon: April, 7am – 9am

Snake: May, 9am – 11am

Horse: June, 11am – 1pm

Goat: July, 1pm – 3pm

Monkey: August, 3pm – 5pm

Rooster: September, 5pm – 7pm

Dog: October, 7pm – 9pm

Pig: November, 9pm – 11pm

How to Use the Chart

Each of the animals is said to have two close friends and one deadly enemy. The two close friends are identified on the chart by counting round four animals in each direction from your own sign; the deadly enemy is the animal directly opposite yours. The two other signs that make up that particular element group are not too good to associate with either. Once you know what each animal represents you can use that information to plan better, more rewarding and fulfilling lives for yourself and your family.

A close group of friends will often find that there are three or four signs predominating. Sometimes there are more than this, which is accounted for by the subtle influence of the elements of each sign.

year charts

Each of the animals has five different and distinct personalities depending on which element governs it – and that depends on the year in which you were born. Look up your birth year and read the introduction to that animal, and then read about the individual characteristics of the animal governed by the relevant element.

The Rat

The Ox

The Tiger

The Hare

The Dragon

The Snake

The Years and Their Signs

Year	From – to	Aspect	Element	Animal
1900	31 Jan 1900 – 18 Feb 1901	Yang	Metal	Rat
1901	19 Feb 1901 – 7 Feb 1902	Yin	Metal	Ox
1902	8 Feb 1902 – 28 Jan 1903	Yang	Water	Tiger
1903	29 Jan 1903 – 15 Feb 1904	Yin	Water	Hare
1904	16 Feb 1904 – 3 Feb 1905	Yang	Wood	Dragon
1905	4 Feb 1905 – 24 Jan 1906	Yin	Wood	Snake
1906	25 Jan 1906 – 2 Feb 1907	Yang	Fire	Horse
1907	3 Feb 1907 – 1 Feb 1908	Yin	Fire	Goat
1908	2 Feb 1908 – 21 Jan 1909	Yang	Earth	Monkey
1909	22 Jan 1909 – 9 Feb 1910	Yin	Earth	Rooster
1910	10 Feb 1910 – 29 Jan 1911	Yang	Metal	Dog
1911	30 Jan 1911 – 17 Feb 1912	Yin	Metal	Pig
1912	18 Feb 1912 – 5 Feb 1913	Yang	Water	Rat
1913	6 Feb 1913 – 25 Jan 1914	Yin	Water	Ox
1914	26 Jan 1914 – 13 Feb 1915	Yang	Wood	Tiger
1915	14 Feb 1915 – 2 Feb 1916	Yin	Wood	Hare
1916	3 Feb 1916 – 22 Jan 1917	Yang	Fire	Dragon
1917	23 Jan 1917 – 10 Feb 1918	Yin	Fire	Snake
1918	11 Feb 1918 – 31 Jan 1919	Yang	Earth	Horse
1919	1 Feb 1919 – 19 Feb 1920	Yin	Earth	Goat
1920	20 Feb 1920 – 7 Feb 1921	Yang	Metal	Monkey
1921	8 Feb 1921 – 27 Jan 1922	Yin	Metal	Rooster
1922	28 Jan 1922 – 15 Feb 1923	Yang	Water	Dog
1923	16 Feb 1923 – 4 Feb 1924	Yin	Water	Pig
1924	5 Feb 1924 – 24 Jan 1925	Yang	Wood	Rat
1925	25 Jan 1925 – 12 Feb 1926	Yin	Wood	Ox
1926	13 Feb 1926 – 1 Feb 1927	Yang	Fire	Tiger
1927	2 Feb 1927 – 22 Jan 1928	Yin	Fire	Hare
1928	23 Jan 1928 – 9 Feb 1929	Yang	Earth	Dragon
1929	10 Feb 1929 – 9 Jan 1930	Yin	Earth	Snake
1930	10 Jan 1930 – 16 Feb 1931	Yang	Metal	Horse
1931	17 Feb 1931 – 5 Feb 1932	Yin	Metal	Goat
1932	6 Feb 1932 – 25 Jan 1933	Yang	Water	Monkey
1933	26 Jan 1933 – 13 Feb 1934	Yin	Water	Rooster
1934	14 Feb 1934 – 3 Feb 1935	Yang	Wood	Dog
1935	4 Feb 1935 – 23 Jan 1936	Yin	Wood	Pig
1936	24 Jan 1936 – 10 Feb 1937	Yang	Fire	Rat
1937	11 Feb 1937 – 30 Jan 1938	Yin	Fire	Ox
1938	31 Jan 1938 – 18 Feb 1939	Yang	Earth	Tiger
1939	19 Feb 1939 – 7 Feb 1940	Yin	Earth	Hare
1940	8 Feb 1940 – 26 Jan 1941	Yang	Metal	Dragon
1941	27 Jan 1941 – 14 Feb 1942	Yin	Metal	Snake
1942	15 Feb 1942 – 4 Feb 1943	Yang	Water	Horse
1943	5 Feb 1943 – 24 Jan 1944	Yin	Water	Goat
1944	25 Jan 1944 – 12 Feb 1945	Yang	Wood	Monkey
1945	13 Feb 1945 – 1 Feb 1946	Yin	Wood	Rooster
1946	2 Feb 1946 – 21 Jan 1947	Yang	Fire	Dog

馬

The Horse

羊

The Goat

猴

The Monkey

雞

The Rooster

犬

The Dog

豬

The Pig

Year	From – to	Aspect	Element	Animal
1947	22 Jan 1947 – 9 Feb 1948	Yin	Fire	Pig
1948	10 Feb 1948 – 28 Jan 1949	Yang	Earth	Rat
1949	29 Jan 1949 – 16 Feb 1950	Yin	Earth	Ox
1950	17 Feb 1950 – 5 Feb 1951	Yang	Metal	Tiger
1951	6 Feb 1951 – 26 Jan 1952	Yin	Metal	Hare
1952	27 Jan 1952 – 13 Feb 1953	Yang	Water	Dragon
1953	14 Feb 1953 – 2 Feb 1954	Yin	Water	Snake
1954	3 Feb 1954 – 23 Jan 1955	Yang	Wood	Horse
1955	24 Jan 1955 – 11 Feb 1956	Yin	Wood	Goat
1956	12 Feb 1956 – 30 Jan 1957	Yang	Fire	Monkey
1957	31 Jan 1957 – 17 Feb 1958	Yin	Fire	Rooster
1958	18 Feb 1958 – 7 Feb 1959	Yang	Earth	Dog
1959	8 Feb 1959 – 27 Jan 1960	Yin	Earth	Pig
1960	28 Jan 1960 – 14 Feb 1961	Yang	Metal	Rat
1961	15 Feb 1961 – 4 Feb 1962	Yin	Metal	Ox
1962	5 Feb 1962 – 24 Jan 1963	Yang	Water	Tiger
1963	25 Jan 1963 – 12 Feb 1964	Yin	Water	Hare
1964	13 Feb 1964 – 1 Feb 1965	Yang	Wood	Dragon
1965	2 Feb 1965 – 20 Jan 1966	Yin	Wood	Snake
1966	21 Jan 1966 – 8 Feb 1967	Yang	Fire	Horse
1967	9 Feb 1967 – 29 Jan 1968	Yin	Fire	Goat
1968	30 Jan 1968 – 16 Feb 1969	Yang	Earth	Monkey
1969	17 Feb 1969 – 5 Feb 1970	Yin	Earth	Rooster
1970	6 Feb 1970 – 26 Jan 1971	Yang	Metal	Dog
1971	27 Jan 1971 – 15 Feb 1972	Yin	Metal	Pig
1972	16 Jan 1972 – 2 Feb 1973	Yang	Water	Rat
1973	3 Feb 1973 – 22 Jan 1974	Yin	Water	Ox
1974	23 Jan 1974 – 10 Feb 1975	Yang	Wood	Tiger
1975	11 Feb 1975 – 30 Jan 1976	Yin	Wood	Hare
1976	31 Jan 1976 – 17 Feb 1977	Yang	Fire	Dragon
1977	18 Feb 1977 – 6 Feb 1978	Yin	Fire	Snake
1978	7 Feb 1978 – 27 Jan 1979	Yang	Earth	Horse
1979	28 Jan 1979 – 15 Feb 1980	Yin	Earth	Goat
1980	16 Feb 1980 – 4 Feb 1981	Yang	Metal	Monkey
1981	5 Feb 1981 – 24 Jan 1982	Yin	Metal	Rooster
1982	25 Jan 1982 – 12 Feb 1983	Yang	Water	Dog
1983	13 Feb 1983 – 1 Feb 1984	Yin	Water	Pig
1984	2 Feb 1984 – 19 Feb 1985	Yang	Wood	Rat
1985	20 Feb 1985 – 8 Feb 1986	Yin	Wood	Ox
1986	9 Feb 1986 – 29 Jan 1987	Yang	Fire	Tiger
1987	30 Jan 1987 – 16 Feb 1988	Yin	Fire	Hare
1988	17 Feb 1988 – 5 Feb 1989	Yang	Earth	Dragon
1989	6 Feb 1989 – 26 Jan 1990	Yin	Earth	Snake
1990	27 Jan 1990 – 14 Feb 1991	Yang	Metal	Horse
1991	15 Feb 1991 – 3 Feb 1992	Yin	Metal	Goat
1992	4 Feb 1992 – 22 Jan 1993	Yang	Water	Monkey
1993	23 Jan 1993 – 9 Feb 1994	Yin	Water	Rooster
1994	10 Feb 1994 – 30 Jan 1995	Yang	Wood	Dog
1995	31 Jan 1995 – 18 Feb 1996	Yin	Wood	Pig
1996	19 Feb 1996 – 7 Feb 1997	Yang	Fire	Rat
1997	8 Feb 1997 – 27 Jan 1998	Yin	Fire	Ox
1998	28 Jan 1998 – 15 Feb 1999	Yang	Earth	Tiger
1999	16 Feb 1999 – 4 Feb 2000	Yin	Earth	Hare
2000	5 Feb 2000 – 23 Jan 2001	Yang	Metal	Dragon
2001	24 Jan 2001 – 11 Feb 2002	Yin	Metal	Snake
2002	12 Feb 2002 – 31 Jan 2003	Yang	Water	Horse
2003	1 Feb 2003 – 21 Jan 2004	Yin	Water	Goat
2004	22 Jan 2004 – 8 Feb 2005	Yang	Wood	Monkey
2005	9 Feb 2005 – 28 Jan 2006	Yin	Wood	Rooster
2006	29 Jan 2006 – 17 Feb 2007	Yang	Fire	Dog
2007	18 Feb 2007 – 6 Feb 2008	Yin	Fire	Pig

the animal signs
the animal signs

the animal signs

The ancient Chinese sages believed that the universe was exactly 3,600 years old, and they divided this time into 300 60-year cycles, which they considered the perfect human lifespan. Each human cycle was divided by the five elements to give 12 years, which were originally referred to as the Twelve Earthly Branches. Eventually these acquired the characteristics of 12 distinct animals. Although, according to legend, the zodiac animals were chosen by the Buddha, it is thought that the names arrived in China from Turkey or Central Asia, possibly not until after astrological studies reached their peak during the period of the Han dynasty (200 BC–AD 200).

Many of the qualities attributed to the animals differ markedly from Western ideas of their characters. The rat, for instance, has a largely negative image in the West, and you may not welcome the idea of such an animal presiding over your life. However, in Chinese astrology the rat is seen as hard-working, loyal to its partner and a good and responsible parent. The snake is regarded not as treacherous or dangerous, but as wise, sophisticated, well-organized and good at solving problems.

The animal signs do not just govern the years. They are also each allotted a month and a time of day over which they preside. So, for instance, you would not be just a tiger, the animal corresponding to your birth year. You might also show some of the characteristics of a monkey if that animal ruled the month in which you were born, and perhaps a goat according to your time of birth. Each of these animals would bring their own qualities to your astrological chart.

The same qualities apply to each animal whether it is the year, month or time of day you are considering. Their combination makes you unique. Your year animal is the outer you – the part seen by the outside world. Your month animal (known as your lunar animal) is you in relationships and love – your inner animal of the heart. And finally, your time of day animal is the real you – the dark, secret animal that you do not show to the rest of the world.

A Chinese astrologer draws up a personal horoscope using the exact moment of your birth, not just the year. Traditionally, before the arrangement of a Chinese marriage, an astrologer would check on the compatibility of the two people concerned, using additional information such as the birth dates of their parents. The descriptions of the animals on the following pages include notes on each animal's compatibility with the other signs.

the rat

Rats are cheerful and industrious. They bounce back quickly from setbacks and even when down they manage to keep smiling. Because of their reputation for being self-motivated they are often mistrusted, but they provide well for their family and make loyal partners and good parents. They love to haggle for bargains and genuinely adore collecting money. Rats do always have a hidden agenda and fend primarily for themselves.

RAT CHARACTERISTICS

Rats do not have a wider social conscience. They look after their own first and foremost. They are passionate and sentimental, and regard a close, big family, well provided for, as their paradise. Rats like company and are not given to much introspection. They can be very generous to their loved ones and have good taste. They may also be very practical, and are able to cope with most tasks quite easily.

Love, Sex and Relationships

Rats are sentimental, sensual and warm lovers. They will go out of their way to please their lovers and like to take the initiative when it comes to seduction. They are naturally faithful but need to be kept interested. As rats are naturally curious, spicing up your love-making with dark secret places, candlelight, good wines and plenty of surprises will ensure a rat stays with you forever. Allow it to be boring and the rat will vanish.

Business, Friends and Children

Rats are the hard-working entrepreneurs of the animal kingdom, and are clearly focused on money and success. They are outwardly charming and quick, and can fool people into thinking that they have the best interests of others at heart, but that is far from the truth. Rats are only interested in themselves and what they can acquire, steal, buy, obtain and accumulate. They hate to fail at anything and will always strive for success, measuring that success by how much they have acquired in material terms. This

The rat likes secret meetings and intrigue, and will indulge in illicit affairs and dangerous liaisons if they get bored.

doesn't make rats bad people – merely greedy. They can turn any situation to their own advantage. Despite these traits, rats are usually popular and genuinely well liked, and usually have many friends. They adore their own children.

	Years of the Rat	Characteristics	Careers
	1900 • 1912	Curious	Auctioneer
		•	•
	1924 • 1936	Intelligent	Money lender
		•	•
	1948 • 1960	Practical	Lawyer
		•	•
	1972 • 1984	Passionate	Antique dealer
		•	•
	1996 • 2008	Self-interested	Car salesperson
		•	•
Element: *Water*	2020 • 2032	Sentimental	Financial adviser

Water Rat

This intuitive, adventurous rat likes to travel, but once it finds a safe haven, it will settle and won't be shifted. The water rat is creative, enjoys literature, and is a good diplomat.

Wood Rat

Although hard-working and successful, this is the least dynamic of the five rats and can be indecisive and prone to worry.

Fire Rat

This quick-witted, passionate rat has a flair for business, and the energy and enthusiasm to match. Unless it learns to curb its recklessness, it can be rather dangerous.

Earth Rat

This serious, prudent rat likes practical problems with practical solutions. Although a bit of a plodder, it is usually successful, and makes a good accountant or financial adviser.

Metal Rat

Strong, with fixed ideas, this rat can be stubborn, although it is helpful and hard-working. An ambitious rat, with the ability to see things through, it will be successful in all it undertakes.

All rats like to travel, but they also enjoy homecomings and don't like to be away from their families for long periods of time.

The rat likes to be part of a big, sociable family.

Rat Compatibility Chart

RAT WITH:

RAT	A good combination as rats need a lot of attention – and are capable of giving lots in return. These two do well together in business or a relationship.
OX	A well-balanced and harmonious partnership. The ox is a good listener and the rat will entertain him or her extremely well.
TIGER	As neither of these two knows how to compromise, this combination will create sparks and the relationship will be stormy.
HARE	The rat is a control freak while the creative and intuitive hare dislikes control of any sort. Not a good combination.
DRAGON	A good relationship despite the apparent differences. Each will support the other in their schemes and will be able to give the other the attention they crave.
SNAKE	The snake's love of secrets and mysteries will inflame the rat to fits of jealousy and distrust. Not a good combination.
HORSE	Neither partner will get a word in edgeways – but if either can learn to listen the relationship does have potential.
GOAT	If the rat is allowed to control and be in charge then this could be a successful union. However, if the goat wants any freedom, the relationship is doomed.
MONKEY	These two characters are similar in personality and do well together. They are both starters rather than finishers and so will need to make allowances for that to do well together.
ROOSTER	With two control freaks, this combination just can't work. Neither partner will be interested in the other and both will demand to be in charge.
DOG	A good team. The rat's control and the dog's loyalty make a good combination, although they both like to talk a lot so the relationship could be a noisy one.
PIG	If the rat can earn it, the pig can spend it. As long as both know where they stand, this is a good partnership.

the ox

The gentle giant of the animal world, the ox is a patient, kind character who takes responsibilities seriously, and expects everyone else to do so as well. The fact that they often don't puzzles the ox, who derives a lot of pleasure from doing things the right way – actually their own way. Oxen can be a bit set in their routines. They like to get up early and get on with their work, and they are tidy and well-organized.

OX CHARACTERISTICS

The ox is a determined character with boundless energy and enormous capacity for hard work. Totally reliable, an ox friend will always be there for you. Also patient, consistent and conscientious, an ox can sometimes be a bit dull and will occasionally need livening up. Basically happy, with few worries, the ox occasionally suffers from irrational fears, and needs lots of exercise and fresh air to prevent introspection. Oxen like to be appreciated and have their advice taken seriously. This is a sensible, sober, traditional type with an understanding of good old-fashioned virtues and hardly a vice at all.

Love, Sex and Relationships

Being wary of emotion and too much excitement, the ox is careful to avoid falling in love. But once an ox does fall in love, it's for life. Just don't expect too much romance – the ox is too down-to-earth for that and, being straightforward about sex, regards it as a practical necessity.

Business, Friends and Children

In business the ox can be ruthless and efficient, preferring to get on with the job in hand and hating any waste of time, energy or money. Ox personalities make good parents as they have infinite patience and kindness. They also have many true friends who know they can depend on the ox in times of trouble. The ox is a very stable animal, and children, business partners and friends can all rely on the ox with total confidence.

All oxen know how to work hard, but the earth ox is the hardest worker of them all.

Element:
Water

Years of the Ox	Characteristics	Careers
1901 • 1913	Reliable	Gardener
1925 • 1937	Purposeful	Judge
1949 • 1961	Patient	Teacher
1973 • 1985	Conscientious	Estate manager
1997 • 2009	Determined	Chef
2021 • 2033	Faithful	Police officer

Water Ox

The diplomatic ox knows how to listen and makes a good counsellor. Advice is freely given when asked for, and is usually good
advice – especially about matters relating to love.

Wood Ox

Blessed with a sense of humour, this laughing ox can be very
witty. It is more adaptable than the other ox types, with a need
to try new things, but the wood ox also has a volatile temper.

Fire Ox

Unpredictable and dangerous, this is the bull in the china shop.
When it has its head down and is working, the fire ox is fine, but
once it becomes bored or restless it can be extremely volatile.

Earth Ox

Earth oxen are resourceful and reliable. They make good
researchers and scientists. They don't like to take risks and are
careful and methodical. They accumulate great wealth through
their hard work and endeavours.

Metal Ox

With considerable talents for organization, this very serious ox
makes a good office manager or a writer of business books.
When a metal ox gives advice you'd better listen, for it knows
what it is talking about, especially when it comes to business.

Choose a water ox to talk to when you need a sympathetic ear.

The ox applies itself to its work and is hard-working and methodical.

Ox Compatibility Chart

Ox with:

RAT	Well balanced and harmonious. The ox is a good listener and the rat will entertain them both extremely well.
OX	Neither one of these two will have anything to say, and they will suffer each other in silence. This is not a good partnership.
TIGER	Unless the tiger allows the ox to be in control and set the rules this combination can't work. As tigers don't give in easily, expect fireworks.
HARE	The hare has a natural optimism that won't suit the ox, who is pessimistic by nature. These two are badly suited.
DRAGON	A powerful combination. The ox can curb the dragon's impetuosity, and if they work as a team they can achieve anything together.
SNAKE	A good long-lasting and stable relationship. The snake understands the ox and will encourage them to lighten up – the ox gives the snake stability.
HORSE	This is not a good combination. The ox is thorough and methodical, while the horse is impulsive and rash. These two will irritate each other continually.
GOAT	These two won't agree on anything, and the ox will be appalled by the goat's apparent lack of morals.
MONKEY	The monkey constantly seeks change and the ox hates it. This combination can't work under any circumstances.
ROOSTER	The rooster sets things in motion and the ox will see them through. A good combination.
DOG	If both partners share the same goals, this can be a good partnership, but in business rather than love.
PIG	The ox will never tolerate the pig's spending habits, and the pig will consider the ox dull. Not a promising union.

the tiger

Rash, impulsive and dynamic, tigers don't know how to sit still, and take fearsome risks. But if you need a hero, then a tiger will do fine. Tigers like to take on the cause of the underdog and will fight against any injustice imaginable. They are invariably charming and persuasive. They are born leaders, not because of any natural leading abilities, but because they can talk anyone into following them – no matter how ill-advised the project may be.

TIGER CHARACTERISTICS

The tiger is one of the most tenacious characters in the Chinese zodiac and very little will daunt tigers – or keep them down for long – they will always bounce back. They are not invulnerable, however, and need lots of emotional support, as they are basically insecure and can feel unloved.

Love, Sex and Relationships

Tigers have infinite resources of energy and imagination and will inevitably tire any lover they tangle with. They are promiscuous and have absolutely no moral sense whatsoever, with no compunction about finding new excitement once the current relationship has begun to fade. They are great romantics and fall in love easily and often. They do have a great capacity for intense relationships and are devastated when these fall apart, even if they are the cause. A tiger in love can be a rogue or simply perfect – and you'll never know which sort you are getting until it's too late.

Business, Friends and Children

Tigers are loners with few really good friends, but those they do have they keep for life. They make good parents; not because they set good examples, but because children just adore these exciting and charismatic personalities. They can be very strict and demanding, and do tend to expect a lot of their offspring. In business, tigers are adventurous speculators, full of new ideas. They are good at starting new projects with enthusiasm and energy, but they hate routine and get bored easily.

The metal tiger protects itself well – it can be ruthless and shouldn't be crossed, but is a pussy cat at heart.

Element:
Wood

Years of the Tiger	Characteristics	Careers
1902 • 1914	Daring	Film star
	•	•
1926 • 1938	Passionate	Army officer
	•	•
1950 • 1962	Heroic	Writer
	•	•
1974 • 1986	Tenacious	Athlete
	•	•
1998 • 2010	Reckless	Politician
	•	•
2022 • 2034	Foolish	Restaurateur

Water Tiger

Possessing a greater sense of moral responsibility than the others, this calm tiger will often set a good example and be fair and just. It can be a bit pompous, though, and is very self-assured.

Wood Tiger

This social big cat is the life and soul of the party, full of bright, entertaining ideas, but it's all a front – this tiger is deeply insecure and feels unloved a lot of the time.

Fire Tiger

The quickest and most ferocious of the tigers, the fire tiger races everywhere as if it were on fire, which internally it may well be. It needs to learn to slow down and relax or it will burn out early.

Earth Tiger

A tiger of extremely good taste, this self-indulgent character recognizes quality and likes to enjoy all the fine things in life. It can run to fat if not careful, as it does enjoy good food and fine wines.

Metal Tiger

This roaring tiger is the most opinionated of all. Very ambitious, it can be ruthless about its career. Don't stand in the way of a metal tiger and never invest in any of its schemes. This is a tiger for whom the word "diplomacy" simply doesn't exist.

The earth tiger is the refined tiger of good taste – it can also be rather self-indulgent though.

Children adore the tiger personality – and tigers are very fond of children too.

Tiger Compatibility Chart

TIGER WITH:

RAT	As neither of these two knows how to compromise, this combination will create sparks and the relationship will be stormy.
OX	Unless the tiger allows the ox to be in control and set the rules, this combination can't work. As tigers don't give in easily, expect fireworks.
TIGER	Expect a lot of heat – the heat of passion and ferocious lust. These two will fight and reconcile, laugh and love – a lot.
HARE	The hare makes a good meal for the tiger unless it learns to move fast to stay out of trouble. Although not a good combination, it can work.
DRAGON	Excitement and fun all the way. Dramatic and volatile. A super-charged dynamic team who together can move the earth.
SNAKE	The snake thinks the tiger is over-emotional, while the tiger distrusts the snake's secretive ways. This relationship is bound to end in disaster.
HORSE	A good combination. The tiger will respect the horse's loyalty and the horse will love the tiger's impulsiveness.
GOAT	Could be good together in bed, but there is not a lot else going for them. This partnership is not recommended for business.
MONKEY	As neither will compromise, this is not a good combination. Both suffer ego problems and neither will understand the other at all.
ROOSTER	In spite of the fact that these two will bicker and quarrel, criticize and argue, this match is quite a good one.
DOG	The dog is clever enough to handle the tiger, so these two will do extremely well together.
PIG	These two blame each other when things go wrong and aren't really suited.

the hare

Intuitive, psychic, sensitive and creative, hares care about others. They are lone souls who feel the pain of the world and often try hard to put it right. They love mysteries and hidden knowledge, and are seekers after Truth. Invariably calm and moderate, quiet and refined, hares like to know secrets, which they are capable of keeping. They make good counsellors and clairvoyants. They are eloquent, with good taste and a strong sense of style.

HARE CHARACTERISTICS

Hares like to express their emotions and can be volatile if roused by cruelty or suffering. They have a strong sense of fair play but like to break rules themselves, and they can be arrogant, seeing themselves as a little superior to others. Hares possess genuine intuitive powers and need a calm stable atmosphere to thrive.

Love, Sex and Relationships

Hares get hurt easily, often in love, so they can be very wary of becoming involved. Considerate, gentle lovers, with a true sense of kindness and romance, they will listen to a lover's problems and needs and do what they can to meet them. Hares are traditional and reserved in their sexual habits and are easily frightened by too much tension or intrigue. They prefer a romantic candlelit supper with their true love to an affair or a one-night stand. They are very moral and can be prudish.

Business, Friends and Children

Because of their sensitive nature and inherent good taste, hares will thrive in any business where they can use their flair for style. They suffer in routine jobs and need to work for themselves. They have many friends, but are likely to feel let down by all of them because no one can meet the high standards that hares set. As parents, hares are wonderfully calm and kind. They are not very good with rowdy or badly behaved children, though, and can be very strict. They do inspire children to work hard, however, and children will adore them.

The hare parent is very loving, calm and kind.

Element:	Years of the Hare	Characteristics	Careers
	1903 • 1915	Intuitive	Accountant
		•	•
	1927 • 1939	Sensitive	Pharmacist
		•	•
	1951 • 1963	Caring	Historian
		•	•
	1975 • 1987	Stylish	Art collector
		•	•
	1999 • 2011	Calm	Librarian
Wood		•	•
	2023 • 2035	Creative	Diplomat

Water Hare

Doubly intuitive and doubly sensitive, the water hare can take on too much of others' troubles and get bogged down in suffering. It is prone to irrational fears and can become reclusive and withdrawn. It needs to be livened up occasionally.

Wood Hare

Truly artistic with immense creativity, this hare is good with anything that lets it express emotion – poetry, literature, painting. It is the most adventurous hare, with a flair for exotic travel.

Fire Hare

This passionate hare has a very strong social conscience, works tirelessly for the good of the world and is good in political debates. It is very expressive and people will listen, and quite rightly so for it does know what's what.

Earth Hare

This serious, studious, hard-working, quiet hare gets on with the job in hand and possesses a fine set of moral principles. It makes a good judge or social worker. This is a sensible, pragmatic, realistic and down-to-earth hare who sets achievable targets.

Metal Hare

Ambitious, with courage and perseverance, this least emotional of the hares will rise to lofty heights in any field where its vision and confidence can be put to good use.

The wood hare likes culture, art and travel – an adventurous and exotic hare.

The earth hare is studious and hard-working.

Hare Compatibility Chart

HARE WITH:

RAT	The rat is a control freak while the hare dislikes control of any sort, so this is not a good combination at all.
OX	The hare has a natural optimism that won't suit the ox, who is pessimistic by nature. These two are badly suited.
TIGER	The hare makes a good meal for the tiger unless it learns to move fast to stay out of trouble. Although not a good combination, it can work.
HARE	These two understand each other perfectly which can make the union very good – or very bad. They will both walk away when things go badly.
DRAGON	The hare helps calm the dragon and they work well together as a team, especially as business partners.
SNAKE	With a lot in common, these two have a natural affinity. Not a lot of passion though.
HORSE	The horse is too impulsive and the hare too thoughtful – they will irritate each other. Not a good combination.
GOAT	As long as nothing goes wrong these two are harmonious and beautiful together. At the first sign of trouble they will not support each other, however.
MONKEY	These two characters are so completely alien to each other, a union can't work. They have nothing in common.
ROOSTER	The hare's stand-offishness will infuriate the rooster and the rooster's arrogance will alienate the hare. Not a good combination.
DOG	A nice combination. They understand and respect each other so the partnership works extremely well.
PIG	For some strange reason, these two always seem to get on well. Perhaps it is true that opposites attract – it is in this case.

the dragon
Big, bright and bold, the dragon is life's good luck symbol. Dragons are glorious and mythical, confident and glamorous. They can also be vain and arrogant, but are so wonderful that you cannot help but be impressed. They are also fickle and erratic, they love new things but quickly tire of them. Dragons are usually extremely energetic, full of life and fun. They like to be surrounded by friends and admirers, sycophants and lovers.

DRAGON CHARACTERISTICS
Dragons are bright, showy creatures, always buying new clothes. They have an endless enthusiasm for life, parties and kindness. Although they are generally very friendly and considerate of others, you must be careful never to anger one because you won't like the results – dragons really do breathe fire.

Love, Sex and Relationships
Dragons need more lovers than the world can provide. They get bored so quickly that anyone falling for a dragon had better know it will be short-lived. The only really true companion with any chance of a long-term relationship for a dragon is another dragon. If a dragon does ever fall in love – which may be a rare thing indeed – it will worship the loved one with a deep, possessive, jealous love that is almost suffocating in its intensity. Dragons like sex, a lot, and will wear out any lover, except another dragon, with their demands.

Business, Friends and Children
Dragons perform well in any field where they can be adored and admired – acting is good for them and they also make good fashion designers, impresarios and producers. They are best heading a large corporation rather than working for someone else. Dragons will have many friends. They never think badly of children, but they try to avoid having any of their own – they simply can't stand the mess and noise. Other people's children are fine for a while as they can be handed back to their parents.

The glamorous dragon likes to be the centre of attention.

	Years of the Dragon	Characteristics	Careers
	1904 • 1916	Successful	Managing director
		•	•
	1928 • 1940	Independent	Tycoon
		•	•
	1952 • 1964	Confident	Film star
		•	•
	1976 • 1988	Energetic	Producer
		•	•
	2000 • 2012	Kind	President
		•	•
Element: *Wood*	2024 • 2036	Ostentatious	Fashion designer

Water Dragon

The idealistic water dragon can be very egotistical – it alone has the solution to the world's problems and can't understand why we aren't all listening to it.

Wood Dragon

This beautiful dragon is an exquisite beast that is admired by everyone. A great trend-setter and leader of fashion, it is aloof and sophisticated, cool and stylish.

The dragon loves dressing up and showing off.

Fire Dragon

Bigger and brighter than any other dragon, this one is very entertaining, witty and warm-hearted, but it does possess a temper.

Earth Dragon

The only dragon who can work as part of a team, the earth dragon is more realistic and self-knowing than the other types. It is very conservative and traditional.

Metal Dragon

The theatrical metal dragon, although bombastic and opinionated, is very entertaining and colourful – truly eccentric.

The earth dragon can be an effective teamworker.

Dragon Compatibility Chart

DRAGON WITH:

RAT	A good relationship despite the apparent differences. Each will support the other in their schemes and will be able to give the other the attention they crave.
OX	A powerful combination. The ox can curb the dragon's impetuosity, and if they work as a team they can achieve anything together.
TIGER	Excitement and fun all the way, dramatic and volatile. A super-charged dynamic team who together can move the earth.
HARE	The hare helps calm the dragon and they work well together as a team, especially as business partners.
DRAGON	If they can learn to work together (unlikely) they get on very well. If not they fight (more likely).
SNAKE	A mystic union. They are both reptilian and each understands the other well. A good combination.
HORSE	These two are a lot of fun together although they will fight and argue a lot. A very interesting pairing.
GOAT	Goats are attracted to dragons but get hurt in the process as dragons fail to see them – the indifference is hurtful.
MONKEY	A brilliant combination. These two are both clever, versatile and active. They both like to live by their wits and together they make a formidable partnership.
ROOSTER	A dramatic but good partnership. They both have big personalities but are sufficiently different to make the union interesting.
DOG	Bad news. These two positively dislike each other on sight. The relationship can't and won't work.
PIG	The dragon inspires the pig and the pair bounce off each other. The pig can get roasted, though, so it should keep a little in reserve.

the snake

Snakes are the philosophers and deep thinkers of the Chinese zodiac. They are mysterious, sensual, indulgent and sophisticated. They can be cruel and remote, but if given the right start in life (a sound education and good moral guidance) they are extremely practical. Snakes can see solutions where others might not even see a problem. They have wisdom, exploring the deep mysteries of life, and are clever without ever appearing to work.

SNAKE CHARACTERISTICS

Snakes are perpetually curious about the world and love to investigate anything esoteric and secret. They are incredibly well-organized and will always find quick and efficient ways to get things done – they never seem to have to make very much effort in their accomplishments, but one of their best points is that they always finish the tasks they begin.

Love, Sex and Relationships

Snakes are sensuous and enjoy their relationships. They delight in sex, particularly in all its darker aspects, and can be considered extreme by some. They can be cold lovers, though, because they have an innate aloofness and remoteness that could be considered arrogant. It's not arrogance, however, it's just that they are always busy thinking. Snakes are passionate and very intense. They feel things deeply and analyse everything. They can become too intense and overwhelming. They love to flirt and will often be unfaithful, but it's not because they don't love their partners – they just need to check occasionally that their old magic charm is still working.

Business, Friends and Children

Snakes do well in any field of research, science and discovery. They make good scientists, philosophers and lecturers. They acquire a large number of friends because they do like to hear confessions and have secrets revealed to them – they are brilliant listeners. As parents, snakes can be rather vague, as they find

The sinuous snake moves with ease and grace. It is languid, stylish and effortlessly clever.

it hard to concentrate on the trivia of children's needs, but they do inspire children to become educated and thoughtful and they will teach their children to love books. They are generally kind parents, if a little abstracted and remote.

Element:
Fire

Years of the Snake	Characteristics	Careers
1905 • 1917	Mysterious	Professor
	•	•
1929 • 1941	Sophisticated	Astrologer
	•	•
1953 • 1965	Practical	Psychologist
	•	•
1977 • 1989	Indulgent	Interior designer
	•	•
2001 • 2013	Wise	Personnel officer
	•	•
2025 • 2037	Organized	Philosopher

Water Snake

This honest snake possesses integrity and a well-developed sense of fairness and honour. The ability to see other people's problems from all points of view makes this snake a wise counsellor or a good arbitrator.

Wood Snake

Imaginative and creative, the wood snake is often a writer with a wonderful sense of beauty and finesse. It may appear lazy, however, and can be self-indulgent.

Fire Snake

A dynamic snake with boundless energy, this snake isn't quite so philosophically minded as the others, and can do well in public life as it has a clearer appreciation of reality.

Earth Snake

A friendly, harmonious snake with a great love of culture and social functions, this is the party snake with charm, wit and sophistication. It is amazingly vague and forgetful.

Metal Snake

This strong, perfectionist snake is serious and hard-working with a quick sharp brain. The metal snake is invariably honest and moral – even to the point of being fanatical.

Wood snakes have a natural sense of beauty and finesse.

Fire snakes are dynamic and can fire people's imaginations.

Snake Compatibility Chart

SNAKE WITH:

RAT	The snake's love of secrets and mysteries will inflame the down-to-earth rat to fits of jealousy and distrust. Not a good combination.
OX	A good long-lasting and stable relationship. The snake understands the ox and will encourage it to lighten up – the ox gives the snake stability.
TIGER	The snake thinks the tiger is over-emotional, while the tiger distrusts the snake's secretive ways. This relationship is bound to end in disaster.
HARE	With a lot in common, these two have a natural affinity. Not a lot of passion though.
DRAGON	A mystic union. They are both reptilian and understand the other well. A good combination.
SNAKE	They get along fine but shouldn't get romantically involved – they're both much too jealous.
HORSE	A good combination. They spark each other off and as long as they both know what the other is doing they get on fine.
GOAT	Only in exceptional circumstances can this combination work. It's much more likely to end in indifference as the two have different agendas.
MONKEY	These two mistrust each other, are jealous of each other and have no real understanding of the other. Yes, the relationship is doomed to failure.
ROOSTER	Despite their differences these two get along just fine. There is friction but it is manageable.
DOG	The dog trusts the snake, which suits the snake just fine. An unlikely combination but one that works.
PIG	These two never make a good combination and will never be able to see the other's point of view.

the horse
Friendly and communicative, horses are great givers and incurable gossips. They are kind, generous, supportive and well-liked, and appreciate openness and honesty. Horses talk a little too much, however, and they're always so cheerful it can be irritating. They can also be somewhat irresponsible and careless. As long as they're in the limelight, everything is fine, but if they lose your attention they can become sulky and bored.

HORSE CHARACTERISTICS

Horses shy away from anything subversive or dark and prefer plain-speaking to any coded messages – they're not very good at picking up hints. This doesn't mean that they're thick-skinned, just unaware of subtleties: they have little notion of tact or discretion. They can be a bit boisterous and overpowering, but they have hearts of gold and are genuinely nice people.

Love, Sex and Relationships

A happy horse is one that is in love – and horses are usually happy. They do love to be in love. They are big softies, very romantic and charming. They can be impatient as lovers, however, and have a tendency to rush things. Although enthusiastic and exciting lovers, they can become bored easily if the magic and romance begins to wane. They enjoy all the physical aspects of love-making and are energetic lovers.

Business, Friends and Children

Horses and money never go well together. Horses are frivolous and, as they never think of tomorrow, they do not accumulate any savings. Being creative and talented, anything to do with business does not appeal to them. They are social and popular – especially among other horses, and have many friends – good ones. They can be very good with children as long as they are outdoors and where nothing can get broken. Horses are notoriously clumsy and their boisterousness can sometimes frighten timid children.

The horse is eternally cheerful and well-meaning, but not very perceptive of other people's feelings.

Element:	Years of the Horse	Characteristics	Careers
Fire	1906 • 1918	Hard-working	Reporter
	1930 • 1942	Friendly	Inventor
	1954 • 1966	Generous	Technician
	1978 • 1990	Talkative	Comedian
	2002 • 2014	Cheerful	Wine expert
	2026 • 2038	Boisterous	Racing driver

Water Horse

This truly artistic horse is very communicative and witty, with a tremendous sense of fun. Although very charming, the water horse can be a little insensitive.

Wood Horse

Calmer and more reserved than the water horse, the wood horse is slightly gullible and can get teased a lot. But it is always jolly and rarely gets depressed.

Fire Horse

In Chinese horoscopes this extreme horse is either feared or famed. It either rises to incredible heights or sinks to the lowest depths. The fire horse year occurs only every 60 years and the next isn't until 2026.

Earth Horse

This is a stable and conventional horse with traditional views and a rigid set of morals. Earth horses can be rather pompous but do pay attention to detail and are relatively well-organized.

Metal Horse

Headstrong and easily bored, this horse needs a lot of excitement and passion. It is the Don Juan of horses and needs many admirers and lovers.

The boisterous horse enjoys rough-and-tumble play and gets on well with children.

The water horse is very communicative and often has many friends.

Horse Compatibility Chart

HORSE WITH:

RAT	Neither partner in this noisy combination will be able to get a word in edgeways – but if either can learn to listen, the relationship does have potential.
OX	The ox is thorough and methodical, while the horse is impulsive and rash. These two will irritate each other continually. Not a good combination.
TIGER	A good combination. The tiger will respect the horse's loyalty and the horse will love the tiger's impulsiveness.
HARE	Not a good combination. As the horse is too impulsive and the hare too thoughtful they will irritate each other.
DRAGON	These two are capable of having a lot of fun together although they will inevitably fight and argue a lot. A very interesting pairing.
SNAKE	These two spark each other off and as long as they both know what the other is doing they get on fine. A good combination.
HORSE	Not a very emotional pairing but one that can work extremely well. They both love their freedom and trust one another.
GOAT	These two can learn a lot from one another, and they have the potential to give a lot to each other as well. A good combination.
MONKEY	After the initial cut and thrust for dominance has taken place, this is a very long-term, lasting relationship.
ROOSTER	The horse hates arguing and the rooster loves arguing, so these two can never really get on.
DOG	A brilliant relationship under any circumstances. These two understand each other almost telepathically.
PIG	The horse's popularity will enhance the pig's social standing – which the pig will appreciate. A good combination.

the goat

Of all the animal signs the goat is the one best able to live in the moment. Goats don't fret about the past and they don't worry about the future. They are relaxed, happy-go-lucky creatures who like to enjoy what they have now rather than strive for what might be. Goats are creative and friendly and certainly like to meet people and talk a lot. They are kind, honest and imaginative. Nothing is too much trouble if it helps other people.

GOAT CHARACTERISTICS

Goats can be fiercely independent creatures and they hate being hemmed in or having their freedom curtailed. They need new people, fresh horizons and new experiences and excitements. They like to partake of all that life has to offer – they are perpetually curious and this can lead them into trouble.

Love, Sex and Relationships

Goats have a capacity for making lovers feel very special – as if they are the only and true one. However, the goat will have many lovers and will try very hard never to settle down or be in a permanent relationship, which looks like a trap to them. They are adventurous when it comes to sex and like a lot of variety and experimentation. Goats aren't particularly moral and shouldn't be judged by conventional standards.

Business, Friends and Children

Because of their charm and elegance, people are sometimes jealous of goats, but those who know goats well realize they have a good heart and care a lot about their friends. Goats in business are rare – in fact goats who work hard for long hours are rare. They are not lazy; just not motivated by money. They can be extremely busy and industrious when they want to be, but the project has either to be creative or to benefit humankind in some way. Children adore goats as they will take time and trouble to talk to them without patronizing, and will go out of their way to treat them with the same respect as an adult.

Untroubled by needless worries, goats like to relax and be peaceful. They have a certain elegance and style.

	Years of the Goat	Characteristics	Careers
	1907 • 1919	Adaptable	Television presenter
		•	•
	1931 • 1943	Sexy	Sex counsellor
		•	•
	1955 • 1967	Creative	Musician
		•	•
	1979 • 1991	Friendly	Artist
		•	•
Element:	2003 • 2015	Independent	Garden designer
		•	•
Fire	2027 • 2039	Curious	Actor

Water Goat

This conservative goat dislikes change or any other kind of upheaval in its life. It is very sympathetic and has a tendency to take the world's worries on its own shoulders. It is sensitive and emotionally perceptive in its dealings with others.

Wood Goat

A very sensitive, generous goat with great compassion, its impressive talents for inspiring other people would make it an excellent leader of a new religion.

Fire Goat

Courageous and intuitive with a good sense of drama, this goat would make a fine actor. It can be reckless and foolhardy, however, and should never be trusted with large amounts of money – its own or anyone else's.

Earth Goat

This goat likes fine, rare and beautiful objects and enjoys good art. It would make an excellent art critic or collector of antiques.

Metal Goat

Determined and ambitious, the metal goat enjoys a particularly thick skin and is impervious to criticism. This goat will have a go at anything relentlessly.

The earth goat has a very discriminating eye and likes to be surrounded by unusual and beautiful objects.

Water goats are sensitive and do not like change, so farming is a good career as it keeps them close to nature.

Goat Compatibility Chart

GOAT WITH:

RAT	If the rat is allowed to control and be in charge then this could be a successful union. However, if the goat wants any freedom, the relationship is doomed.
OX	These two won't agree on anything, and the ox will be appalled by the goat's apparent lack of morals.
TIGER	Could be good together in bed, but there is not a lot else going for them. This partnership is not recommended for business.
HARE	As long as nothing goes wrong these two are harmonious and beautiful together. At the first sign of trouble they will not support each other, however.
DRAGON	Goats are attracted to dragons but are likely to get hurt in the process as the egotistical dragons fail to see them – the indifference is hurtful.
SNAKE	Only in exceptional circumstances can this combination work. It's much more likely to end in indifference as the two have different agendas.
HORSE	These two can learn a lot from one another, and they have the potential to give a lot as well. A good combination.
GOAT	One of this pair will need to take control – and that's the problem. Neither is any good at being in charge and together they will go nowhere.
MONKEY	This isn't a bad partnership. The monkey motivates the goat and the goat curbs the monkey's excesses.
ROOSTER	The rooster will never allow the goat time off, while the goat will be irritated by the rooster's flamboyance.
DOG	These two can tolerate each other well but there's little passion between them and little understanding.
PIG	Each of these leads the other astray, which can be fine but is not really conducive to a lasting relationship.

the monkey
Inquisitive, bright, energetic and highly competitive, the monkey is the liveliest of the animal signs – full of new ideas. Monkeys are very good at manipulating other people. They make fine leaders – as long as people realize that where they are being led is entirely at the whim of the monkey – and they always have their own agenda. Monkeys have quick, sharp brains and are usually extremely sharp-witted, though not necessarily wise.

MONKEY CHARACTERISTICS
Monkeys are social creatures who love having lots of people around them. They are also, however, independent characters, and are always optimistic. They like to take risks and will always rise to a challenge – or a dare. The monkey is loud and communicative, full of itself and very entertaining.

Love, Sex and Relationships
Monkeys have voracious appetites, both for relationships and for sex. They enjoy the challenge of new conquests and love the experience of being in love. They seem to achieve their best potential while in a relationship, but their interest, as in all things, will quickly turn to something – or someone – else if their interest isn't kept up – they need fresh excitement continually. Monkeys have no moral code and will stray at any opportunity that arises. They hate conflict in any relationship and will run at the first sign of trouble.

Business, Friends and Children
Monkeys collect large numbers of friends, and small children will follow them to the ends of the earth. Business partners will drop them quite quickly, however, when they attempt to follow any of the monkey's crazier schemes – of which there will be many. Monkeys and money are easily separated. Monkeys change careers often and quickly, as they hate routine. They can shine in any occupation where they can use their wits, be entertaining and not work too hard. The monkey is, by nature, quite indolent.

The monkey is a mercurial trickster, full of ideas and schemes.

	Years of the Monkey	Characteristics	Careers
	1908 • 1920	Quick-witted	Journalist
		•	•
	1932 • 1944	Entertaining	Teacher
		•	•
	1956 • 1968	Inquisitive	Entrepreneur
		•	•
	1980 • 1992	Energetic	Travel writer
		•	•
	2004 • 2016	Manipulative	Therapist
		•	•
Element: Metal	2028 • 2040	Optimistic	Publicist

Water Monkey

You won't ever understand this secret monkey, full of hidden agendas and complex mysteries. It is a monkey from another planet. It is affectionate but keeps its distance. It can be a worrier and take slights to heart.

Wood Monkey

A truly resourceful monkey, very talented, artistic and creative, this is the cleverest of all the monkeys. It is the friendliest monkey too, and is very warm and lovable.

The energetic monkey likes plenty of stimulation and adventure, and relishes an element of danger.

The monkey is quick-witted and can use this to its advantage. As it thinks well on its feet, it could do well in buying or selling.

Fire Monkey

This passionate lover monkey is very dynamic, charming and ruthless, and needs more lovers than there are available. It is very dangerous, but very attractive.

Earth Monkey

More harmonious than the other monkeys, this is the great communicator. It is extremely witty and very funny, although its humour can verge on the cruel. Its parodies are extremely accurate, if unkind.

Metal Monkey

This monkey loves to take risks. It may well be a gambler and may be the only monkey that can make money. It is very independent, hates to be tied down and will escape any traps laid for it.

Monkey Compatibility Chart

MONKEY WITH:

RAT	These two characters are similar in personality and will do well together. They are both starters rather than finishers and so will need to make allowances for that to do well together.
OX	The monkey constantly seeks change and the ox hates it. This combination can't work under any circumstances.
TIGER	As neither will compromise, this is not a good combination. Both suffer ego problems and neither will understand the other at all.
HARE	These two are so completely alien to each other, a union can't work. They have nothing in common.
DRAGON	These two are both clever, versatile and active. They both like to live by their wits and together they make a formidable partnership. A brilliant combination.
SNAKE	These two mistrust each other, are jealous of each other, and have no real understanding of the other. Yes, the relationship is doomed to failure.
HORSE	After the initial cut and thrust for dominance has taken place, this is a very long-term, lasting relationship.
GOAT	These two can learn a lot from each other, and they have the potential to give a lot as well. A good combination.
MONKEY	Too much rivalry. Too much competition. This combination could settle into a team but it is unlikely.
ROOSTER	If they share any interest they can get along – but that is not really a basis for a love match.
DOG	If these two have any common interests they get on well but basically they do not make a good combination.
PIG	A good team for indulgence. They both like pleasure and excitement and get on well together. Not a good combination though if there are any serious problems.

the rooster
Roosters like to show off. They are flamboyant, colourful people with outgoing, friendly personalities. They are good communicators and enthusiastic. They do like to be independent although they are fond of their families. They can be very entertaining as they are never still or quiet, but most of their stories will be about their own prowess. Roosters are far more sensitive than you'd ever know, and they can be deeply hurt by criticism.

ROOSTER CHARACTERISTICS

Roosters put great store by education, and will read and learn a lot by themselves. They often know more than you think, although they don't like to appear too clever. They often play the part of the buffoon when they don't need to – it's just another way of getting attention.

Love, Sex and Relationships

Love is a serious business for roosters and when they take a partner they expect it to last – for life. They are not, however, necessarily completely faithful themselves but they do expect their partners to be. They are dramatic and exciting lovers and have endless sexual energy but little imagination. Roosters expect a lot from their partners, and can be quite hard to be with in a relationship, especially as they don't like to give too much away about themselves in return.

Business, Friends and Children

Roosters like to be surrounded by people, but while they certainly have many acquaintances, they don't really ever open up sufficiently for close friendships to develop. Roosters adore children and can give them considerable attention while still working hard themselves – a unique skill. Roosters have an infinite capacity for hard work which makes them very popular with employers. They love a challenge and will often enter an occupation for which they seem unsuited, and will then slog heroically away at it until it is conquered.

Though outgoing and apparently confident, the rooster can be insecure deep down.

	Years of the Rooster	Characteristics	Careers
	1909 • 1921	Protective	Engineer
		•	•
	1933 • 1945	Honest	Beautician
		•	•
	1957 • 1969	Flamboyant	Surgeon
		•	•
	1981 • 1993	Entertaining	Company director
		•	•
	2005 • 2017	Sensitive	Hairdresser
Element:		•	•
Metal	2029 • 2041	Noisy	Public relations

Water Rooster

One of the few roosters that can work in a team, this is a sympathetic, caring rooster who takes on world causes. A kinder, calmer rooster.

Wood Rooster

With masses of enthusiasm, the very extroverted wood rooster can be highly creative but is also prone to live life excessively and may overdo anything it takes on.

Fire Rooster

This dramatic, flamboyant rooster can be very successful if it can curb its aggressive streak. It has a unique ability to be able to see into the future and plan accordingly, which can make it a bit reckless as it thinks it is all-knowing.

Earth Rooster

The earth rooster is a very determined, blunt rooster of few words. It can be disliked for its forthright opinions but it is usually right. It takes its responsibilities seriously and can be ambitious.

Metal Rooster

As it sets very high standards indeed, this rooster won't tolerate fools and expects everyone to live up to its ideals. It is rather inflexible and can suffer as a result. This rooster needs to learn to relax and will find times when it needs to be on its own.

The metal rooster sometimes needs periods of quiet, solitary contemplation.

Roosters can give children a lot of attention but are able to work hard at the same time.

Rooster Compatibility Chart	
ROOSTER WITH:	
RAT	With two control freaks, this combination just can't work. Neither partner will be interested in the other and both will demand to be in charge.
OX	The rooster sets things in motion and the ox will see them through. A good combination.
TIGER	In spite of the fact that these two will bicker and quarrel, criticize and argue, this match is quite a good one.
HARE	The hare's stand-offishness will infuriate the rooster and the rooster's arrogance will alienate the hare. Not a good combination.
DRAGON	A dramatic but good partnership. They both have big personalities but are sufficiently different to make the union interesting.
SNAKE	Despite their differences these two get along just fine. There is friction but it is manageable.
HORSE	The horse hates arguing and the rooster loves arguing, so these two can never really get on.
GOAT	The rooster will never allow the goat time off, while the goat will be irritated by the rooster's flamboyance.
MONKEY	If they share any interests they can get along but that is not really a basis for a love match.
ROOSTER	This couple will bicker and criticize each other but they can get on well – they can also fight. Overall, not really a good match.
DOG	The dog will eventually get bored waiting for the rooster to calm down, and the rooster will be irritated by the dog's patience. Not a good combination.
PIG	Although different, these two can be friends. They share similar interests and can have an interesting, if passionless, relationship.

the dog

Of all the Chinese animals the dog is the friendliest and kindest. Dogs are here to serve us all and they love being of use. It is no accident that the dog was chosen to represent this group of people, for the dog is a firm, dutiful, noble beast indeed. Dog people are unselfish and moral. They love to be with other people and are extremely honest, trustworthy and tolerant. They are easy to take advantage of, and they can overdo their good aspects.

DOG CHARACTERISTICS

Dogs are eager to please, perhaps too ready to help, too anxious to serve. They can also be a bit unadventurous and can suffer from a kind of victim mentality where everything that goes wrong is endured with fatalism and stoicism. If left to their own devices they can run wild – they need to be supervised and led.

Love, Sex and Relationships

Although dogs are into romance and love in a big way, they enjoy friendly relationships much more. They seek companionship rather than sex and would be quite happy to keep all their affairs platonic. Their need to please, however, makes them good lovers as they go out of their way to be approved of and praised. They are quite faithful but do need a lot of reassurance that they are still loved. They can be very jealous and suspicious lovers, which can lead them to destroy a relationship unintentionally.

Business, Friends and Children

Children would rather be with a dog than any other zodiac sign. Dogs are big kids at heart themselves. They have few really close friends but everyone loves a dog in their own way. Dogs are very outgoing, social people who need constant contact and company. This is probably best seen in their love of children, whom they adore. Dogs are extremely hard workers and can rise to any challenge. They work well in teams and will shoulder responsibility well. They don't particularly like to lead and need to be encouraged by their colleagues, and given specific tasks.

Dogs understand loyalty better than any other animal.

	Years of the Dog	Characteristics	Careers
	1910 • 1922	Loyal	Critic
		•	•
	1934 • 1946	Trustworthy	Lawyer
		•	•
	1958 • 1970	Friendly	Doctor
		•	•
	1982 • 1994	Kind	Priest
		•	•
	2006 • 2018	Unselfish	Professor
Element:		•	•
Metal	2030 • 2042	Fatalistic	Charity worker

Water Dog

The water dog has the happiest, most easy-going character. It likes being outdoors and makes a good farmer or gardener. This is a more relaxed, charming dog, and one who can afford to be slightly more liberal with other people than the other types.

Wood Dog

The creative wood dog is extremely talented and has the ability to put together a most wonderful home environment for itself and its family. It is very intuitive and can empathize with the needs and problems of others.

Fire Dog

This mad, flamboyant and colourful dog is loved and idealized for its kindness and warmth. It is brilliant with children, as it has infinite patience and resources when dealing with them and with all its friends and acquaintances. In spite of making time for everyone, it still has time to pursue an unusual career.

Earth Dog

Well-balanced and with materialistic ambitions, the earth dog is capable of considerable success in fulfilling them. It is especially well suited to a career in the world of entertainment, as it possesses natural charisma.

Metal Dog

This guard dog can bite. It is never happier than when prowling around, making sure that everything is safe for others. Although it can be very principled, strong and determined, it is still essentially a dog and likes to be liked.

The relaxed and happy water dog finds satisfaction in creative outdoor pursuits such as gardening.

Dogs are keen on romance and the world of love, but enjoy friendly relationships as much, if not more.

Dog Compatibility Chart

DOG WITH:

RAT	A good team. The rat's control and the dog's loyalty make a good combination. They both like to talk a lot though.
OX	If both partners share the same goals, this can be a good partnership, but in business rather than love.
TIGER	The dog is clever enough to handle the tiger, so these two will do extremely well together.
HARE	A nice combination. They understand and respect each other so the partnership works extremely well.
DRAGON	These two positively dislike each other on sight. The relationship can't and won't work.
SNAKE	The dog trusts the snake, which suits the snake just fine. An unlikely combination but one that works.
HORSE	A brilliant relationship under any circumstances. These two understand each other almost telepathically.
GOAT	They can tolerate each other well but there's little passion between them and little understanding.
MONKEY	If these two have any common interests they get on well but basically they do not make a good combination.
ROOSTER	The dog will eventually get bored waiting for the rooster to calm down, and the rooster will be irritated by the dog's patience. Not a good combination.
DOG	They may love each other forever – or fight on sight. The union is risky but worth it if it works.
PIG	No real conflicts, although the pig's spending habits may baffle the thrifty, honest dog.

the pig

Pigs love pleasure, but what their pleasures are may be hard for other signs to understand. Pigs need to know all about themselves emotionally, which can result in emotional turmoil. But they do have big hearts and care a lot about other people. They are very forgiving and always seek a quiet and peaceful life, even to the point of being withdrawn from the mainstream, preferring instead to stay at home and indulge themselves.

PIG CHARACTERISTICS

Pigs are moral beasts; clean in their habits and avoiding anything dark or dangerous. They expect others to follow their strict virtuous guidelines and are surprised when they don't. Pigs have good common sense and their advice will often be sought and followed. Pigs are natural mediators and diplomats.

Love, Sex and Relationships

Pigs will do anything to keep their partners happy – until they have had enough and then they become boars. A roused pig is dangerous and should be avoided. Pigs are happy in love and need a good partner who will allow them the space and freedom to explore their own emotional needs – they will, however, rarely find this. Because of their own inward turning they will often miss the warning signs of a relationship dwindling due to lack of attention.

Business, Friends and Children

Pigs have many friends as they are popular and keep a good table. They love to cook for friends and their advice will often be asked for. Children find pigs a bit hard to take as they can be very strict and set such high standards. A pig in business is a rare sight indeed. Pigs think it better to let others do all the hard work and keep them well supplied with everything they need. Pigs do expect a lot from others, including being looked after. Pigs need security and will plan for it. They don't take risks and they like comfort and harmony in their lives.

Pigs like to roll around in the mud, and can seem rather self-indulgent in their tendency to withdraw into themselves.

Element:
Water

Years of the Pig	Characteristics	Careers
1911 • 1923	Sensual	Chef
1935 • 1947	Eager	Healer
1959 • 1971	Pleasure-seeking	Counsellor
1983 • 1995	Moral	Diplomat
2007 • 2019	Virtuous	Civil servant
2031 • 2043	Self-indulgent	Architect

Water Pig

This self-indulgent pig needs to be got out of bed and made to work hard or it will wallow forever and its love of home may become obsessive, leading to melancholia. In spite of its lazy, good-for-nothing habits, however, this is a charmer.

Wood Pig

Wise and ambitious, this powerful pig can achieve great success, if it is not taken advantage of along the way.

Fire Pig

Brave and adventurous, this pig likes to take risks – although these may initially appear to be small ones, they can eventually lead to dramatic consequences.

Earth Pig

Whatever happens outside, in the big wide world, this prudent, home-loving pig will invariably do whatever is necessary to make sure it is safe and secure inside.

Metal Pig

Witty and entertaining, this party pig doesn't like to stay at home for too long. As long as there are good food and fine wines on your table, you'll not be rid of the metal pig. It is very sociable and friendly – until your cupboard is bare, and then you will find that it will quietly slip away, only to return another day when your stocks are replenished.

Pigs enjoy their home life and like to make it comfortable.

Pigs love entertaining their many friends and are often good cooks.

Pig Compatibility Chart

PIG WITH:

RAT	If the rat can earn it, the pig can spend it. As long as both know where they stand this is a good partnership.
OX	The ox will never tolerate the pig's spending habits, and the pig will consider the ox dull. Not a promising union.
TIGER	These two blame each other when things go wrong and aren't really suited.
HARE	For some strange reason these two always seem to get on well. Perhaps it is true that opposites attract – it is in this case.
DRAGON	The dragon inspires the pig and the pair bounce off each other. The pig can get roasted, though, so it should keep a little in reserve.
SNAKE	These two make a good combination if they ever manage to see the other's point of view.
HORSE	The horse's popularity will enhance the pig's social standing – which the pig will appreciate. A good combination.
GOAT	Each of these leads the other astray, which can be fine but is not really conducive to a lasting relationship.
MONKEY	A good team for indulgence. They both like pleasure and excitement and get on well together. Not a good combination though if there are any serious problems.
ROOSTER	Although different these two can be friends. They share similar interests and can have an interesting, if passionless, relationship.
DOG	No real conflicts, although the pig's spending habits may baffle the poor thrifty dog.
PIG	These two can be friends but nothing more. They both rather like to over-indulge, which isn't an ideal basis for a lasting love affair.

palmistry

palmistry palmistry istry

The "hands-on" approach used in palmistry makes it one of the kindest and friendliest methods of divination. All the time you are looking into the palm to interpret the lines and markings found there, you are touching and holding someone's hand. This intimate and caring gesture can have a profound effect in lifting any personal barriers to communication; it allows the person to feel comfortable and cared-for, enabling them to open up and express whatever is really on their mind at the time. When you are going to read someone's palm, it is important to look at both the hands to judge the various changes that have occurred between child-hood and adult life. The palm-reader reads the major hand (the one used to write with) to find what an individual has made of their life up to the present time, and what is in store for them in the future. The minor hand reveals their past history and family background and shows what talents or assets are inborn.

Choose a setting that is comfortable both for you and the other person. Try to clear your mind, and then look clearly at the hands, always listening to your sixth sense or intuition. You will also find it helpful to have a notebook, a magnifying glass, a ruler, and a pair of compasses. Put them within easy reach so that you do not have to interrupt the reading once it has begun.

Once you have discovered how much infor-mation is on the palm, you will look at hands in a different light. Palmistry is a wonderful way to discover more about yourself and others.

general aspects of the hand

Before studying the lines and markings of the palm itself, some general indications of personality can be drawn from various aspects of the whole hand. This information should be collected as a whole to give you a general picture of the person whose palm you are interpreting. More advanced palmists will also take into consideration the undertones of the skin and the texture of the hand itself.

SHAPE OF THE HAND

Ascertain the overall shape of the hand by holding it up with the palm facing you and using an imaginary outline to gauge its shape.

Pointed or "Psychic" Hand

Narrow hand; middle finger peaks higher than others. These individuals tend to have keen intuitive faculties and a sixth sense. Usually very good-looking, they strive for perfection around them and within themselves.

Conical or "Artistic" Hand

This gently rounded shape is so-called because these people are extremely visual, and artistic; they are sensual by nature. They want to see all the beauty in life, and they see life as something to be enjoyed.

Square or "Useful" Hand

This shape belongs to individuals who need to be needed. They have a logical pattern to their thinking, and usually have a good mechanical sense. They are often very busy physically.

Spatulate or "Necessary" Hand

The palm widens out from a narrow base. These people get things done. They will do whatever is necessary to succeed, and are persistent and bright enough to carry it off. These individuals hate to waste time.

A musician is likely to have a palm longer than the fingers, showing creativity and dexterity.

PROPORTIONS OF THE HAND

Differences in length between the palm and the fingers can usually be seen with the naked eye, but if necessary simply use a ruler to measure the difference. By holding it lengthwise alongside the whole hand you can assess at a glance the proportions of fingers to palm.

Palm is longer than fingers

This indicates people who have difficulty in saying no to their whims; people of ideas and dreams who can conjure up great schemes but need to watch out for the "Oh, I'll put it off until tomorrow" syndrome. They are creative people and are likely to be artists or musicians.

Palm is same length as fingers

Very balanced individuals have this balanced hand. They find it relatively easy to cope with the highs and lows in life and are usually stable in character, both mentally and physically. They are determined individuals who have the ability to see things out to the end and have a logical approach to life. They are very fortunate in that they suffer few health problems.

Palm is shorter than fingers

These individuals will always use their gut intuition to guide them through life. They are very imaginative and sensitive. They have a delicate constitution and may suffer health problems.

Conical hand

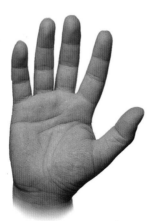

Spatulate hand

Pointed hand

Square hand

FINGER SHAPES

When assessing the shape of the fingers, examine them with the palm facing you, looking only at the overall shape of the fingertips while ignoring the shape of the fingernails. Many people will have a mixture of finger shapes, so look for the shape which occurs most frequently. At this stage you should also take into account the settings, spacings and patterns on the fingers and thumb, all of which are dealt with later.

Pointed fingertips

Finicky, precise personalities, these people have a good eye for colours, shapes and designs. They are refined, with a highly developed aesthetic sense and good taste, which will be evident in their dress and homes.

Conical fingertips

These individuals carry certain instinctive beliefs about themselves and possess a great inner knowledge of other people's circumstances and concerns. They are generally wise souls with a gentle nature, always willing to lend a hand and help out. They are usually very attractive.

Square fingertips

These people prefer to lead a simple life, with simple pleasures to keep them happy. They are excellent workers, who are always able to make money easily, and so do well in the field of business. They are always scrupulously fair in their approach and in their dealings with others.

Spatulate fingertips

Highly intelligent and witty, these people have a dry sense of humour and are mentally versatile. They enjoy travelling. They are very active and will generally go for a career in which they will work non-stop around the clock. They are adaptable, capable of handling most situations and other people.

Most people are likely to have more than one shape of fingertip on their hand. If this is the case, base your reading on the shape which occurs most frequently. Finger shapes (left to right): pointed, conical, square and spatulate.

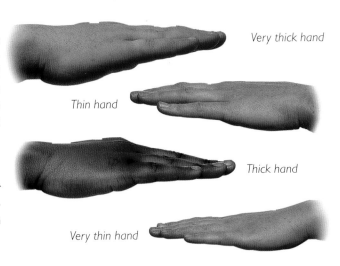

Very thick hand

Thin hand

Thick hand

Very thin hand

HAND THICKNESS

Tilt the hand sideways to judge its depth and suppleness.

Very thick and very hard

These individuals tend to behave in a very rough, tough manner, following their own basic needs and crude thoughts.

Thick and hard

These people have very basic needs: food, shelter and love. Free from ambition, they have no desire to keep up with the rat race.

Thick and medium hard

These people are good workers, always reliable and trustworthy. Life does not come too easily for them, but they usually enjoy it.

Thick and medium soft

These people work hard and play hard; they really want to enjoy themselves with other people. They need to be needed.

Thick and soft

These people are artists, poets or musicians, but are not usually very good workers. They tend to dream and ponder on life.

Thin and very hard

These individuals have strategic skills and can be quite calculating. They may seem cold, but it takes time to get to know them.

Thin and hard

These people tend to be selfish and self-opinionated. They are possessive and stubborn and do not make friends easily.

Thin and soft

These people are always the last to leave a party. They find it difficult to say "no", so they are susceptible to temptations.

Thin and very soft

These individuals have a keen intuition, but tend to focus on the negative, which may lead them to react harshly or snap at others.

the size of the hand

When ascertaining the size of the hand, you should consider it in relation to the person's size and build. Ask yourself if it is in proportion. For example, a small person who has small hands would be considered to have hands of average size. The hands of a tall and broadly built man might be larger, but if they look dainty compared to the rest of his body you should consider them as small.

Very Small Hands

Individuals with hands that are very small in proportion to the rest of their body tend to be free thinkers. They often have a fiercely strong sense of moral politics and will stick firmly to their beliefs and stand up for them. They like to fight for the underdog against dishonesty and injustice. However, this may lead to a tendency not to listen to the other side of a story, so their support can be misguidedly given. If a man has exceptionally small hands, it can indicate that there is a cruel side to his nature.

Small Hands

Individuals who have proportionally small hands are ideas people. They often come up with bright and broad-reaching ideas, but they usually need the support of others to help carry them through to fruition. People with small hands make very good committee members and fundraisers because they possess an ability to gather the support and enthusiasm of others in their endeavours. They are usually very dear and sweet in nature, and would not hurt a fly.

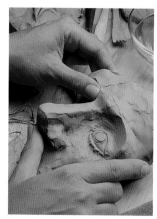

People with large hands are often surprisingly dextrous.

Average Hands

People with average-sized hands are down-to-earth individuals who usually possess good common sense. They have balanced, healthy attitudes and are good-natured. Any mental or physical problems are easily overcome.

Large Hands

People with large hands have a surprising aptitude for doing fiddly things with great patience, and may use this talent to earn their living. They have excellent analytical talents and are mentally strong and good-natured. They can usually be found figuring out detailed projects or pursuing hobbies.

Very Large Hands

These individuals are very bright mentally. They love trivia and mental exercises which sharpen their minds. They can be the mavericks and trendsetters and are unlikely to accept the status quo. They often possess a great strategic ability. They like to be constantly in charge of life, and object to being told what to do.

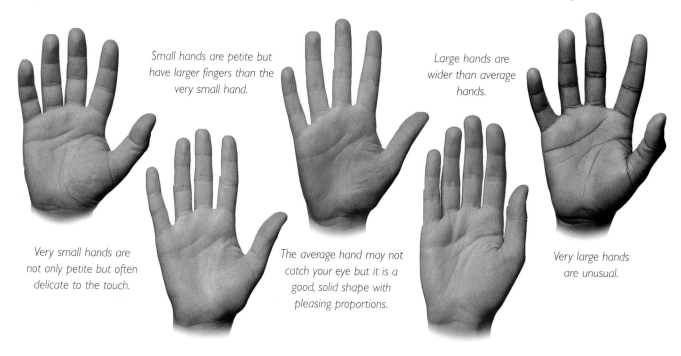

Small hands are petite but have larger fingers than the very small hand.

Large hands are wider than average hands.

Very small hands are not only petite but often delicate to the touch.

The average hand may not catch your eye but it is a good, solid shape with pleasing proportions.

Very large hands are unusual.

elemental hands

There are four basic types of hands, each of which corresponds to one of the four elements: water, air, fire and earth. Assessing this aspect gives an overview of a person's character based on astrological principles. This then complements the detailed interpretation of the palm and fingers made during the reading. The elemental hand often corresponds with the individual's astrological zodiac sign.

Water Hand

The person who has a Water hand has a delicate structure with long fingers and a long palm which features a fine mesh of linear markings. Often, though not always, the water hand belongs to those people born under one of the three water signs: Cancer, Pisces and Scorpio. They possess emotional natures, with very sensitive and sensual personalities. They are often artistic, enigmatic, esoteric and intuitive. The water hand usually accompanies an attractive face with large, intense eyes and soft lips. These people have a love of music, art and culture, and seek relationships: they feel the need to belong to someone or something, in order to be fully content with their lives.

Air Hand

Those people with an Air hand have a robust hand structure with long fingers and a fleshy, though square, palm, with well-defined linear markings. The air hand frequently belongs to those born under one of the three air signs: Libra, Gemini and Aquarius. They are intellectual in their pursuits and possess well-balanced minds. They are literate and not overly sensitive to visual stimuli. They need facts and figures to help guide their decision making, and they look for mental challenges. They are strong-minded individuals with a powerful sense of self. For their relationships to work and not become bogged down or boring, these people need to retain their independence and personal freedom. They need a strong sense of self to be content in life.

Individuals with a Fire Hand tend to be fiery characters who like responsibility as long as it involves action and excitement.

Individuals with an Earth Hand are down-to-earth, reliable characters with a useful ability to detect fakes and swindlers.

Fire Hand

The Fire hand is an energetic hand structure with short fingers and a long palm, and has lively linear markings. Often, though not always, the fire hand belongs to those people born under one of the three fire signs: Aries, Sagittarius and Leo. These individuals have strong instincts, and act on gut feelings. Often they are assertive and quick to rise, but also quick to cool down. They usually prefer action to excuses; they need to be kept busy, otherwise they are easily bored. These people can handle the stresses of a battle but cannot always cope with the more mundane responsibilities of life. They like to be life's leaders and do not enjoy following on behind others.

Earth Hand

The Earth hand is a heavy, thick hand with short fingers and a coarse, square palm; the lines on the palm are few but are deeply incised. The earth hand frequently belongs to people born under one of the three earth signs: Capricorn, Taurus and Virgo. They are well-balanced and logical by nature and make good problem solvers. They have an inherent wisdom. They are sure-footed in their dealings with people and have a useful ability to detect fakes or liars. Once committed to a personal relationship, they are normally very devoted. Earth types need a purpose in life and usually feel a need to be relied upon. They are not afraid of, nor do they mind, good, honest hard work in order to reach their goals.

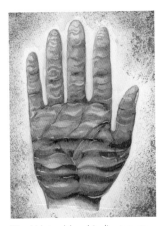
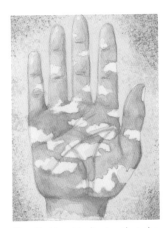

The Water Hand indicates an artistic, sensitive character with strong emotions.

The Air Hand indicates that the character is strong-minded and well-balanced.

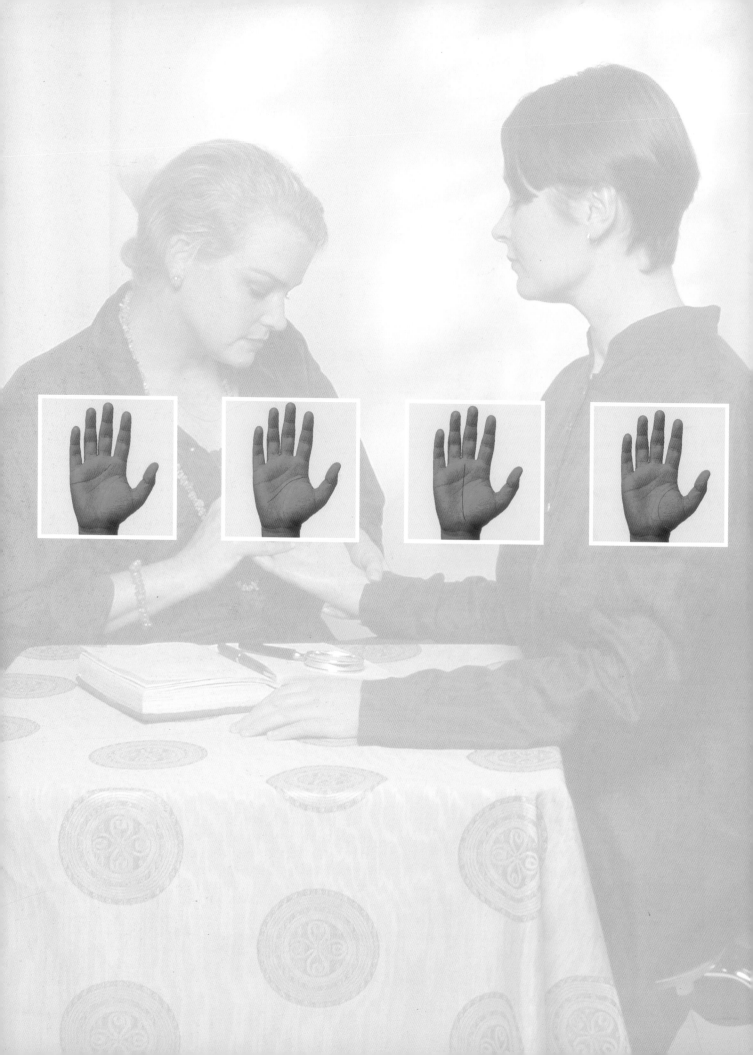

reading the palm
reading the palm

reading the palm

A good palm-reader is one who also brings intuition and common sense to their reading. You are dealing with a whole person, and that includes their feelings. To begin, take a moment before the other person enters the room to clear your mind. Invite the other person in. Focus on your unity with them. Maintain a calm silence until you feel ready to begin. Then explain briefly that the lines and mounts can change, so that everyone has control over their own life. Ask your subject if they are right- or left-handed, and ask their age.

While you are looking at the hands, keep half your attention focused in on your intuition and half of it focused out towards the hands. Ask yourself what the main themes of this person's life are. Scan the hand, noting the relative strength of the mounts and the length and proportions of the fingers. Look for the main lines and any special marks. There are six major lines of the hand. At least three will be found on every hand, but remember that, whether you find only three or all six, the hand must be interpreted as a whole. So, while you are looking at these major lines, you will still be considering the shape and size of the hand, the mounts, other lines, and the fingers. The major lines are normally assessed in their order of importance, which is as follows.

The life line, or "vital line" is read first. It is never absent. Next is the head line or "cerebral line", which deals with the mind. Serious mental illness may be indicated by its absence, although this condition is very rare. The heart line or "mesal line" deals with love and the emotions. The longer the line and the more it reaches towards the Jupiter finger, the longer a relationship is likely to last. Its absence is rare, but it can be a grave

omen. If you do not detect this line, be tactful with your subject and ask a professional reader for advice.

The fate line, or "line of luck", which deals with career and ambition, frequently takes the place of the line of the Sun or Apollo, also known as the "line of fortune and brilliancy". This line deals with luck, talent, and money. The longer it is, the greater the luck. The line of Mercury, or "health line" deals with health issues which may be hereditary. It is often absent, but this is auspicious as it indicates good health.

After looking at, and listening to, everything, take a deep breath and let the information come together naturally in your mind. When you have a general idea of what you're going to say, assess the person and decide on the best way to express yourself. Remember, be kind! Speak clearly, letting your intuition guide you, and ask if they understand you. As long as you touch on the meanings of all the major lines and mounts in the context of the hand, you will do fine. Think carefully and be sure that what you say is exactly what you mean. Open up your intuition and listen to what the palm is telling you.

Ask the person if they have any further questions, and see if the questions can be answered directly from the palm. As long as you make it clear that the hands represent probabilities, not certainties, and that the person's lines can often alter with time, you can answer the questions. If a person asks about death, do not answer the question directly. Above all, take your time and keep yourself open and receptive. Bring the reading slowly to a close. Take time once your client has left to go over the reading in your mind. Was there anything else you could have said?

the life line

The life line is the measure of vitality and life force. It deals with the length and strength of life, family ties and the generalities of life. It is always present in the hand. It starts above the thumb and is then read downwards towards the wrist, where it ends. You may notice one or more thin horizontal lines cutting directly across the life line. These indicate slight obstacles at a given time period.

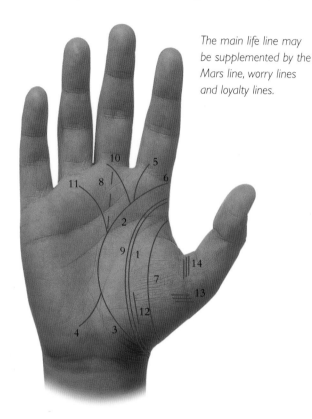

The main life line may be supplemented by the Mars line, worry lines and loyalty lines.

1 Life line close to the thumb
This indicates someone who has a close relationship with their family and is content with family life. They are happy spending time at home, with no great ambition or urge to travel.

2 Life line towards middle of hand
This indicates a person who wants to achieve great things and break new ground. They will have a keen sense of adventure and want to travel.

3 Line ends near thumb side of wrist
When the life line veers around the thumb to end at the side of the wrist, this indicates an individual who yearns for home and wants to end their years on home ground.

4 Line ends towards other side of wrist
When the end of the life line veers away from the thumb towards the opposite side of the hand, this indicates a person who will emigrate, or move away from their family.

5 Line starts at base of Jupiter
When the life line starts below the index finger, the individual seeks a change of lifestyle for the better. They are strong-willed and very ambitious.

6 Line from side of hand near Jupiter
These people are ambitious and will single-mindedly achieve success. They are proud characters who make good leaders.

7 Line cuts close to thumb
This person lives a restricted life under a strong religious or cultural influence, in prison or in the place where they were born.

8 Breaks in the life line
Breaks signify starts and stops in life resulting from big changes such as marriage, divorce, or the death of a close relative.

9 Double life line
This can mean three things: the person may be a twin; they may have a guardian angel or they may lead a double life, such as being a mother during the day and working in a club at night.

10 Effort line
When the life line veers upwards towards the mount of Saturn, a person is working hard and not taking no for an answer. But this does not necessarily mean success.

11 Success line
If the life line veers upward towards the mount of the Sun, it indicates success and good fortune. It may also be a sign of fame.

12 Mars line
This line, running inside the life line, indicates that the person has a guardian angel or protective spirit looking after them.

13 Worry lines
Horizontal lines in the pad of the thumb indicate stresses and worries. The deeper the lines, the more serious the worries. Many faint lines indicate someone who is prone to anxiety.

14 Loyalty lines
Vertical lines creased in the pad of the thumb indicate loyalty to family and friends.

the head line
This line deals with the mind, indicating weak or strong mentalities, possible career directions, and intuitive and creative faculties. Look first to see whether the line is thin and faint, indicating a person who is highly strung, or thick (wide and deep), which is a sign of someone who is methodical. They seem to lack enthusiasm and drive at times; they are solid and sound but stubborn in nature.

1 Line starts high near Jupiter
A head line that starts on the mount of Jupiter, under the index finger, indicates an ambitious individual who is a self-starter and very focused. They can be very competitive and determined in their efforts to achieve their goals in life.

2 Head and life lines tied
This usually indicates an individual beset by doubt and confusion which leads to a lack of independence. They are very involved with the family. They have little self-confidence and doubt their abilities. This may be due to upbringing or early environment.

The head line deals with an individual's strength of character.

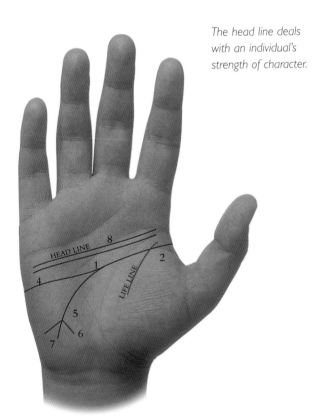

3 Head line separate from life line
When the head line is clearly segregated from the life line, it indicates an individual who possesses great independence and self-will. This is a free thinker who does not follow others but will make their own road in life.

4 Line cuts straight across palm
When the head line touches both sides of the palm, this indicates a self-centred individual who has the ability to stay very focused on their needs and goals. They must have secure material foundations, such as house ownership, insurance policies, and a healthy bank balance. The good news is that they are good citizens and will often give money or time to charity.

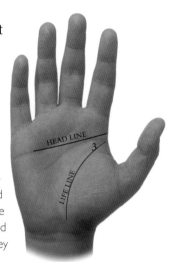

The head line may be positioned separately from the life line.

5 Line dips
A head line that forms an arch, dipping downward into the palm, indicates a very sensitive individual with a highly developed intuition. They are imaginative and perhaps rather eccentric. This may lead them to artistic pursuits or into a profession that involves caring for others.

6 The "writer's fork"
A head line that splits in three directions at the end (like a chicken's foot) indicates an intuitive nature similar to the previous example. People with this characteristic are inclined to communicate cerebral ideas, thoughts and information to others by using their hands. They are likely to be writers, journalists or computer programmers.

7 The "communicator's divide"
When the head line divides into a two-pronged ending, it indicates a person who has great communication skills, and is an able public speaker. They may work in radio or television, as a professional after-dinner speaker or be an actor or singer.

8 The double-headed line
Two head lines lying close together indicate an individual with outstanding mental abilities. The double-headed line is so rare that when it does exist the person is likely to be in a very studious and analytically-driven career, such as an eminent mathematician, scientist or other scholar.

the heart line
This line deals with all matters relating to the heart: love, romantic interests, and relationships with family and friends. It indicates degrees of contentment and happiness in life, as well as the nature of a person's relationships: whether they are likely to be steady or stormy, short-term or long-term. The longer the line, the longer a relationship is likely to last. In general, the heart line deals with a person's emotional and romantic life.

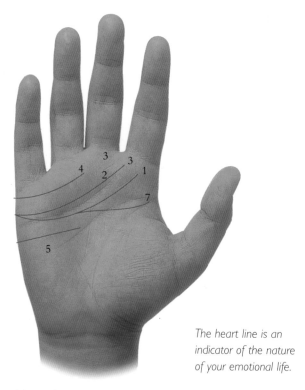

The heart line is an indicator of the nature of your emotional life.

1 Line low in the hand
The heart line starts below the underside of the knuckles in the palm. These individuals are lovers; feminine and romantic, they believe in love and are looking for "fairy-tale" perfection. In matters of the heart they can become perfectionists and expect too much from their partners. This high expectation can lead to them feeling let down.

2 Line high in the hand
The heart line starts on or above the underside of the knuckles in the palm, and appears to rest near the base of the fingers. These individuals are extremely sensitive to what others think of them. As a result they can become quite destructive with their self-criticism. They tend to be very reserved with their emotions.

3 Line veers to middle or index finger
This heart line indicates a dominant and demanding person, who expresses their emotions bluntly. Someone whose line veers towards Saturn (under the middle finger) will have a very contented family life. They keep family members close to them, both physically and in their heart. Veering towards Jupiter (under the index finger) the heart line indicates a person who is very successful in love. They will end their years in love, and the love they bestow will be returned.

4 Short, high line
This person's loyalties and morals are expendable: they believe that sex is the answer. If they are feeling unloved or neglected, or if someone pays a lot of attention to them, they can give themselves over too easily.

5 Short, low line
This individual cannot be faithful: they think that sex is a game or a sport. They are very self-indulgent and assume that if they do not talk about their activities then no harm will be done. So, they are quite self-deceptive too.

6 Line touches head and life lines
When the heart line drops down to touch the head and life lines, it indicates a person who wants the best of both worlds: to be happy both at home and at work. They need love but also have a strong sense of independence. At times they can feel divided between family and career. More often they will find a way to juggle both and find a happy medium in their own way.

7 Line runs straight across the palm
A heart line which runs in an almost straight line right across the palm of the hand indicates a humanitarian with a great sense of purpose in life. This type of person will put a great deal of time and effort into working hard for the good of the community. He or she will experience great luck in life due to their selfless nature.

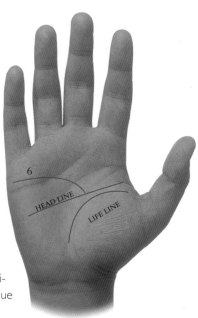

the fate line

This line deals with career, work, ambition, and the direction of a person's life, beginning from their childhood. It also indicates the person's faith in their own abilities. It is read from its starting point at the bottom of the palm, near the wrist, and leads up the palm towards the base of the fingers. It often takes the place of the line of the sun, and ends in varying positions between the index and middle fingers.

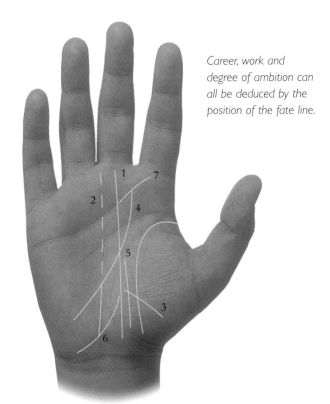

Career, work and degree of ambition can all be deduced by the position of the fate line.

4 Line starts on Lunar mount
When the fate line starts from the side of the palm opposite the thumb, it normally indicates an independent individual who will break away from family traditions. It may also indicate someone who is likely to move overseas to work.

5 Line of milieu
If a separate line runs vertically alongside the fate line for a short distance, it indicates outside pressures or responsibilities. These may be slowing down the individual's way forward, so that they are thwarted in their ambitions.

6 Influence lines
If short lines veer upwards in a feathering motion from the fate line, they indicate positive influences from other people. Feathery lines veering downwards indicate negative influences.

7 Line veers upwards to Jupiter finger
The individual possesses great determination and keen leadership qualities. The will to win is second nature.

Double line
A double fate line means one individual with two careers. They may be running two companies, or have one job in the daytime and a different one in the evening.

1 Fate line runs up middle of palm
This vertical line indicates an individual who has had a keen sense of direction and purpose in their life and career from an early age. It could also indicate that they will pass down their trade or business to their family members.

2 Breaks in the fate line
When the fate line is full of breaks it indicates changes in life and career. These people have never really been able to become fully involved, so may be able to achieve only mediocre success.

3 Fate line begins by veering away from, or touching, the life line
Family commitments were important early in the life of this individual. Before they reach middle-age they will have great family responsibilities or will be heavily involved in a family business. They tend not to want to travel and are inclined to stay close to home in later life.

A keen sense of purpose in life is apparent when the fate line is deep and unbroken up the middle of the palm.

lines of the sun and mercury

Also known as the line of Apollo, the Sun line deals with luck, success in life, talents, and money. It is seldom seen below the heart line. The longer the line, the more luck will be found. Two or three lines together also increase a person's chance of luck and good fortune. The Mercury line is also known as the health or liver line as it deals with health issues, including hereditary ones.

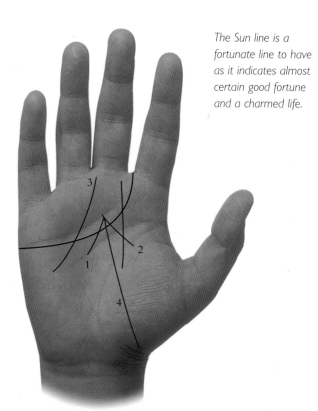

The Sun line is a fortunate line to have as it indicates almost certain good fortune and a charmed life.

MERCURY LINE

The absence of the Mercury line indicates good health.

1 Mercury line cuts across life line

This indicates a weakened constitution. It is a clear sign of hereditary illness such as diabetes, heart disease or arthritis. This individual needs to pay special attention to their health in order to combat the likelihood of this kind of illness. (It must be stressed that this line does not show the possibility of a fatal illness.)

2 Intuition line

A reversed crescent shape indicates a strong sixth sense. It is always present in the hand of the highly intuitive. These are people who have a deep interest in all things esoteric. They are peace-loving and do not like loud noises, big changes or chaos.

3 Mercury line does not touch life line

This is an extremely fortunate line to have in the palm. It indicates very good health and longevity, together with success in business ventures, and good financial fortune.

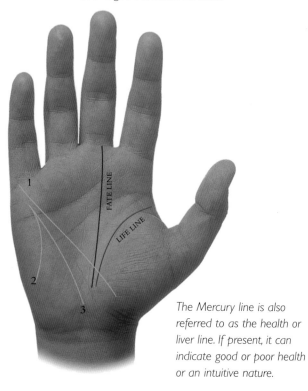

The Mercury line is also referred to as the health or liver line. If present, it can indicate good or poor health or an intuitive nature.

SUN LINE

This line is also known as the line of fortune and brilliancy.

1 Short line

A short Sun line (less than 1cm/½in) indicates an individual who has so far been unable to achieve their goals and dreams.

2 Line curves towards thumb

This individual works very hard to achieve their goals. No one else does the work for them, and, as a result of this self-reliance, they are quite capable of holding on to their achievements.

3 Line curves away from thumb

This line is a good omen if the individual works in the public eye, as it indicates public prestige, and possibly eventual fame.

4 Long line runs vertically

A long Sun line indicates a gilded life, with good luck falling into one's lap. Life will come very easily and successfully.

markings
As you read along the major lines of the palm – the life, head and heart lines – you are likely to come across various markings created by the many small lines that cross or abut them. These may include distinctive shapes, such as stars and squares, which will help you in your reading. It must be said that these markings do not imply anything grave or fatal, but simply indicate stresses or irritations. Indeed, some are signs of protection or good fortune.

Bars and dots
These signify hindrances preventing the individual from moving forward. It will be hard work to recover momentum, and willpower must be kept up throughout this period.

Cross
This is a sign of a more significant or longer-lasting problem such as divorce or the loss of a job or home. On the life line, one cross may indicate a non-fatal accident in early life. Two crosses indicate an individual who is sensuous and willing to learn. Crosses at the end of the life line indicate poverty or ill health in old age.

Square
This wonderful marking represents protection and good health, and indicates being saved at the last minute. A square containing a cross is a sign of preservation: there will be danger but it will not be harmful. Any square on the life line indicates safety.

Chain
This marking indicates confusion, and comes on to the lines when someone is trying to do too much at once.

Island
An island is a sign that the person's energy temporarily diverges in two directions. The mark shows that the individual has bitten off more than they can chew, but also shows they have the ability to pull it all back together. On the life line, islands indicate serious but treatable illnesses.

The islands on the palm offer a temporary respite from a situation.

Tassel
This mark appears at the end of a line and indicates a scattering of the power of the line.

Fork
A fork in a major line shows increased possibilities of success in life, love or career.

Star
On the life line, this can indicate the gain (birth) or loss (death) of a relative. For each gain there is a loss and vice versa.

Circles
On the life line, a circle could indicate problems with the eyes.

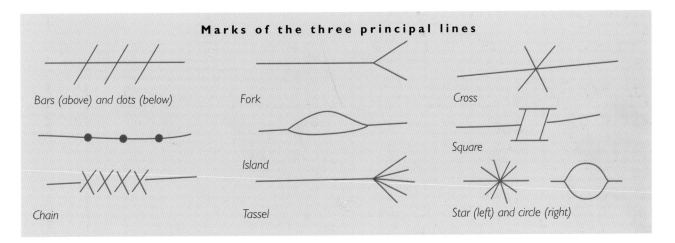

Marks of the three principal lines

Bars (above) and dots (below)

Fork

Cross

Square

Island

Chain

Tassel

Star (left) and circle (right)

lines of special interest

These lines complement the major lines of the palm. They are each unique in their meaning and everyone has at least one, although some people have all of them. They give valuable additional information to the reader about an individual's character, personality and situation, whether it is an indication of courage, psychic ability or a long-lasting romantic commitment.

Line of Mars

Situated on the side of the palm, between the heart and head line, this line indicates great courage. People who have this line make excellent protectors – it is often to be found on courageous military leaders.

LINE OF MARS

Rascettes

These lines, also known as the "Bracelets of Life", are found running across the underside of the wrist just below the palm of the hand, and this is one of the most important areas to check for longevity. The lines can be very faint or very deep, or somewhere in between. Their depth does not matter; it is the number of lines that counts:

1 rascette is equal to 15 to 35 years of life;
2 rascettes are equal to 35 to 55 years of life;
3 rascettes are equal to 55 to 85 years of life;
4 rascettes are equal to 85 to 105 years of life.

THE RASCETTES

5 rascettes are equal to 105 to 135 years of life, though this is very rare except in some parts of the world. The more rascettes a person has on their hand, the longer the life expectancy of that individual.

Girdle of Venus

This can either be one continuous line forming the shape of an upturned crescent moon, or the shape of a saucer; or it can be made up of two lines, one under the other. This marking indicates an individual who can empathize with the deep sorrows of others. Unfortunately, this can lead to them becoming too involved with other people's problems and this can sometimes lead to depression. On a lighter note, these individuals often need to reach for tissues or comforting chocolates when they are watching a sad film on the television and they find this quite enjoyable!

GIRDLE OF VENUS

Sympathy Lines

These lines are always straight and are angled upwards. They indicate a caring nature. They can be found on the hands of nurses, doctors and people who feel a strong need to alleviate pain and suffering in others.

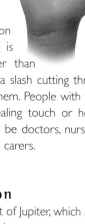

SYMPATHY LINE

Medical Stigmata

This mark, which is found on the hand of a healer, is made up of no fewer than three lines, with a slash cutting through the middle of them. People with these lines have a healing touch or healing hands. They may be doctors, nurses or other professional carers.

MEDICAL STIGMATA

Ring of Solomon

A ring around the mount of Jupiter, which starts at the side of the index finger and sweeps around to end between the first and second fingers, indicates wisdom and a deep interest in the occult, the supernatural and other psychic phenomena. On a less psychic level, the ring of Solomon indicates someone who has good leadership skills, is very good at managing people, and will usually achieve success in life.

RING OF SOLOMON

Ring of Saturn

RING OF SATURN

This semicircular mark beneath the middle finger is rarely found. Whether it is continuous or made up of two or more lines, it seems to isolate and overemphasize the negative Saturnian qualities in a character. Someone with this line will tend to be too serious about life and its problems, and this may lead to depression at times.

LINES OF MARRIAGE

Marriage or Union Lines

There may be one line, indicating one serious involvement and commitment, or two or more lines indicating additional emotional involvements. The longer the line horizontally, the longer the relationship in question will last. Nearly everybody's hand bears at least one of these lines, which represent any serious, committed relationships, not just marriage.

PLAIN OF MARS

This is the area in the centre of the palm of the hand. The plain of Mars shows how sensitive an individual is. In most people, this area will appear concave. If it is slightly raised, or even if it is flat, it is therefore described as "high". Only if it is very markedly indented is it defined as "low".

Average Plain of Mars

When the area is slightly concave, it indicates that the person is balanced emotionally, with good sensibilities and a practical approach to life.

Shallow Plain of Mars

Individuals with this kind of palm can be stubborn, proud and overbearing. They are single-minded and can do one thing at a time very well. Their lack of sensitivity, however, can make them unaware of the problems of other people around them.

Deep Plain of Mars

These individuals will always try to help others, and are highly sensitive to other people's opinions and feelings. They feel other people's pain very personally, and make strong efforts not to upset or offend anyone. If the plain of Mars is too low, it can indicate a tendency towards depression.

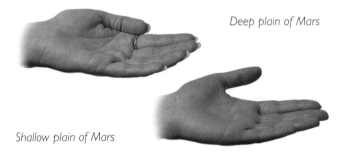

Deep plain of Mars

Shallow plain of Mars

THE PERCUSSIVE OR PALM EDGE

The edge of the palm is a unique area of the hand. It is not a part of the palm itself but rests at the outside edge of the hand. When interpreting this area, you need to take into account that it concerns the aspect of the individual's personality that is projected to the outside world and shows how others may view them. Have the palm facing you when considering this area.

Active Percussive

This person is nearly always busy, with a very active social life. Ever the perfectionist, they search for the best that they can achieve. However, they can have a highly strung nature and be prone to nervousness. These active people are often very physically attractive.

Creative Percussive

This individual tends to be colourful, with a great imagination and creative tendencies; they set their own trends and fashions. They usually have a knack for creating attractive domestic surroundings.

Physical Percussive

This person has excellent physical health with a physique designed for sport and endurance. They are usually involved in physical activities, such as gardening, walking and sport. They need to feel useful and productive.

Independent Percussive

This person is independent and follows their own instincts. They will usually be leaders. They have good intuitive faculties.

Intellectual Percussive

This person prefers mental activity to physical labour. They are problem solvers with an analytical nature. They tend to be physically weak and need to take rests between bouts of exertion.

the mounts of the hand

The mounts are the fleshy mounds present in different segments of the palm. Personality types and even physical traits are indicated by the dominant mount, which is found by looking at the palm from various angles and taking note of which mount is raised highest. As the mounts of Venus and the Moon are the widest, you must compare the height rather than the width to establish dominance.

Predominant Mount of Venus

Physically, the Venusian is likely to be of above average height with a round face, large, clear eyes, a small mouth, thick lips, white teeth and small ears. They will have a high instep, with small, neat ankles and long thighs. Venusian men will usually keep their hair until late in life.

They have a strong and healthy constitution, with a generally cheerful disposition. Venusians are happy and sensually inclined people who love life and social interaction. They are the souls of kindness, and hate quarrelling, strife and warfare.

Predominant Mount of the Moon

Individuals with a predominant mount of the Moon tend to be tall, with a round head and broad forehead. They have very fine hair on their heads and hardly any body hair. Large, yellowish teeth, a small mouth with thick, full lips and large, round bulging eyes are all typical characteristics of these individuals.

Lunar subjects are constantly anxious about their health, which does give some cause for concern. They suffer from poor circulation, have bursts of energy followed by a need for rest, and may also experience problems with their kidneys or their bladder.

Temperamentally, moon subjects are very charming and live their life to the full. They are fond of travel and new and exciting experiences, but also enjoy relaxation. They have a fickle nature, and will tend to start a new job before completing the previous one.

When looking at the mounts on the palm, the reader usually works clockwise, beginning with the mount of Venus.

Alma-Tadema's painting, The Years at the Spring, *has a sensual feel and shows a woman with large, clear eyes and a small, full mouth. She is typical of Venusians, who tend to be life's romantics.*

Predominant Mount of Mars

Martians tend to be of above average height with a strong bone structure; their most noticeable physical characteristic is their prominent cheekbones. They have a large mouth and eyes, thin lips, small, yellowish teeth and small ears. Their head may be proportionally small and the nose may be beak-like. Their voice is powerful and generally attracts attention.

The fiery temperament of the Martian may manifest itself physically in feverishness. With this heated character, Martians are at a great risk of accidental injury when they get into an argument. Martians are amorous individuals by nature with a generous personality, and they enjoy social occasions. They can be domineering, and are often unwilling to listen to reason once they have a fixed idea in their head. Though their hot temper may get them into trouble sometimes, they are courageous but without being vicious.

Predominant Mount of Mercury

The Mercurian is small in stature with good bone structure. They stay young-looking longer than others. Their hair is curly and the skin is soft. They have deep-set, penetrating eyes, a long pointed chin and large hands with long thumbs.

Mercurians do not have a very strong constitution. They are susceptible to weakness of the liver and digestive organs. They often have a nervous temperament.

Quick in thought and action, Mercurians are skilful at all games, good students of mathematics and medicine and excellent in business. They are great judges of human character. Usually of an even-tempered nature, they love the closeness of family life. Their acuity and enjoyment of others makes them natural observers and born actors.

Predominant Mount of the Sun

Those individuals with a predominant mount of the Sun, also known as the mount of Apollo, are usually above average height and have a shapely figure. They tend to be muscular and fit, and are seldom stocky. Their hair is soft and wavy, their mouth is of an average size, and one of their best features is their beautiful, large, almond-shaped eyes.

Apollonians, or solar subjects, have good general health. Their eyes are their weak point. Their below-average eyesight may make them prone to injury stemming from silly accidents like tripping over the carpet.

Solar subjects have versatile minds, with clear, logical thought processes and understanding. They love everything that is beautiful in art and nature but are also, in contrast, very competitive and assertive, always wanting to be ahead of the pack. They make ardent and trustworthy friends, but you should beware of falling out with a solar subject, as they can be bitter enemies.

Sun types can often be found watching people with great interest. Auguste Renoir's painting, Femme à la Rose, *also shows the solar subject's soft hair and large, almond-shaped eyes.*

Predominant Mount of Saturn

Saturnians are tall and thin. They have a long face with a pale complexion. Their eyes are deep set and slope downwards so that they take on a sad appearance. They have a wide mouth with thin lips, a prominent lower jaw, and fine teeth. These people are particularly susceptible to problems with their legs and feet. They are not keen on drinking plain water, so dehydration may be a problem.

Saturnians have a certain sadness in their lives. Conservative and suspicious by nature, they dislike taking orders. They are very prudent, born doubters, good problem solvers, and are interested in the occult sciences. They enjoy country life and love solitude. They spend little and save more, but are passionate gamblers. They like dark colours.

Predominant Mount of Jupiter

Jupiterians have a strong bone structure. They are of average height, usually with attractive curves, and they have a stately walk. They tend to have large, deep-set eyes and thick, curly hair. They have a straight nose, a full mouth, long teeth, a dimple at the base of the chin and ears close to the head. Jupiterian men may lose their hair at an early age. Jupiterians have a tendency to suffer with digestive problems and will often be overweight.

Destined for public life, Jupiterians have confidence in themselves and can be selfish. They like eating out, most social functions and spend money too freely. They love peace, believe in law and order and are, to a degree, conservative.

Alma-Tadema's Portrait of Alice Lewis *captures a Mercurian's intelligent air. Their quick and enquiring mind and even temper makes them excellent judges of other people's character.*

lines and signs on the mounts

Each mount usually features lines and markings such as crosses, squares, or very strong horizontal lines. These signs give the reader a deeper insight into the person's character than can be found by assessing the dominant mount in isolation. When examining the mounts for these lines and signs, use a magnifying glass to give better definition.

The Mounts Combined

Sometimes two mounts are equally raised. This combination gives you an additional insight into the character.

Jupiter and Saturn	Excellent luck ahead.
Jupiter and Sun	Fame and fortune.
Jupiter and Mercury	Love and success in business and science.
Jupiter and upper Mars	Bravery and success as a commander.
Jupiter and Moon	Imagination.
Jupiter and Venus	Pure and respected love towards others.
Jupiter and lower Mars	Cautiousness.
Saturn and Sun	Deep artistic tendencies.
Saturn and Mercury	Love of science and nature.
Saturn and upper Mars	Argumentative temper.
Saturn and Moon	A gift for the occult.
Saturn and Venus	Vanity and pride.
Saturn and lower Mars	A self-critical and reserved nature.
Sun and Mercury	Brilliant talker.
Sun and upper Mars	Leadership instincts.
Sun and Moon	Imaginative.
Sun and Venus	Love of cultural interests.
Sun and lower Mars	Cheerful.
Mercury and upper Mars	Logical and strategic.
Mercury and Moon	Inventive mind.
Mercury and Venus	Prudent in love.
Mercury and lower Mars	Perseverance.
Moon and Venus	Looking for ideal love.
Upper Mars and Venus	Mentality of a soldier.

Venus equals love in many languages, even in palmistry.

MOUNT OF VENUS
Flat, hard mount

This marking indicates an individual who has grown cold to love, due to difficulties in past relationships.

Lines

Two or three lines indicate an individual who suffers with ingratitude in love. They believe that they can always do better, so can be inconstant in relationships.

Strong horizontal lines

This indicates someone who has an overpowering influence on members of the opposite sex.

Mixed lines

This person's disposition will be of a strong and powerfully passionate nature.

Islands

Islands in the lines are a sign of someone who has a tendency to feel guilty in love.

St Andrew's cross

A large cross of this type is a sign that there will only ever be one true love in this person's lifetime. A small cross indicates a very happy and joyous love affair.

Star

A star by the thumb indicates a wonderful, lifelong marriage. However, if it is at the base of the mount it indicates misfortune for the individual due to the opposite sex, such as divorce or a partner's extreme overspending.

Square at base of mount

This person will live a sheltered and protected life.

Triangle

This is the mark of someone who is calculating in love: they may marry for money to get ahead.

Grille

This is a sign of someone with a dreamy and gentle nature.

When we look at the moon, we are captivated by the mysteries of life.

MOUNT OF THE MOON
Long crossed line
A long line with another crossing it shows a tendency to aching bones and rheumatism.

Cross
Indicates a tendency to heart trouble.

Many lines
Indicate a tendency towards insomnia.

Horizontal line
The person will be likely to travel.

A voyage line
An angled, horizontal line which reaches up towards the heart line indicates someone who might suddenly abandon everything to go on a long voyage, or to live in another country for love.

Mixed lines
This, together with a chained heart line, indicates inconsistency in love – the person cannot make up their mind in matters of love.

Cross
This indicates an individual with a superstitious nature. A large cross can indicate someone who has a tendency to brag a lot. On the upper part of the mount, a cross shows a possibility of trouble with the intestines, while in the middle it indicates rheumatism. On the lower part of the mount it can mean trouble with the kidneys or possibly with the bladder.

Square
This mark signifies protection from bad events throughout a person's life. The more squares, the greater the luck.

Triangle
The triangle indicates great inner wisdom and creativity.

Grille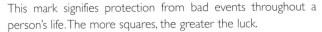
The grille indicates a tendency towards nerve trouble.

MOUNT OF UPPER MARS
One line
Indicates an individual with great courage.

Several lines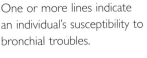
A series of lines in this position indicate someone who may have quite a volatile temper; they can get confused by love, so that they are unable to have a contented relationship.

Horizontal lines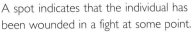
One or more lines indicate an individual's susceptibility to bronchial troubles.

Spot
A spot indicates that the individual has been wounded in a fight at some point.

Circle
This indicates that the person has been wounded in, or around, the eye.

Square
This marking indicates an individual who experiences uncannily good protection from bodily harm, even though they may have put themselves at risk.

Triangle
This indicates an individual who is strategically minded, and is especially adept at military operations.

MOUNT OF LOWER MARS
Ill-formed cross
An irregular cross on this mount may indicate that the individual seriously considered suicide in their youth.

Star on line
A star on a horizontal line running across the mount indicates an individual who has experienced a great misfortune, such as the death of a close relation or a good friend, in their youth. In general, any marking on the mount of lower Mars tends not to be as auspicious as one on the mount of upper Mars.

MOUNT OF MERCURY
One line

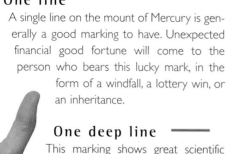

A single line on the mount of Mercury is generally a good marking to have. Unexpected financial good fortune will come to the person who bears this lucky mark, in the form of a windfall, a lottery win, or an inheritance.

MOUNT OF MERCURY

One deep line

This marking shows great scientific aptitude: this person is set to carry out valuable research or make an important scientific discovery.

Three or more lines

These multiple lines indicate an individual who has a great interest in medicine and its related schools of study.

Mixed lines

When the lines are above the heart line, the individual is financially very shrewd and good at saving money, to the extent that they may have great difficulty in spending it.

Mixed lines below the heart line

This is the opposite of the example above. A group of mixed lines below the heart line shows that the individual is so generous that they have a tendency to spend too much on others. They should try to curb their desire to spend.

Cross

This person has a tendency to deceive, though this does not always mean that they are doing so in a negative manner. Sometimes you will see this mark on the palms of actors or sales executives, people who sometimes need to present an image which is not their own. However, people who are prone to lying a great deal can also have this marking.

Star

This individual definitely has difficulty telling the truth. More often than not they will be dishonest in their dealings with other people and in their relationships.

Square

The individual with this marking is blessed. They will be saved or preserved from heavy financial losses. This is a wonderful marking to have in your hand.

Triangle

This individual is shrewd in politics and in their dealings with others. They tend to listen to the other side of an argument first and then respond, and they will usually put their point of view with tact and diplomacy.

Mercury

MOUNT OF THE SUN
One line

This marking indicates the likelihood of gaining great wealth.

Two lines

These lines indicate real talent but without achieving much success.

Many lines

This person has artistic tendencies and may be successful in a creative sphere.

MOUNT OF THE SUN

Cross

This marking indicates success.

Star

The star indicates that fame may be nigh but only after the individual has taken many risks to achieve this goal.

Spot

A spot indicates that a person's reputation is in danger.

Circle

This is a very rare mark and indicates great fame.

Square

The square indicates someone with a great commercial mind.

Triangle

This marking indicates a selfless individual who wants to assist in the success of others.

Grille

The grille can indicate that an individual is inclined to vanity.

Saturn

MOUNT OF SATURN

One line
A single line signifies that an individual will benefit from very good luck.

One long, deep line
A long, deep line indicates a peaceful ending in old age, perhaps passing away quietly while sleeping at home.

Three or more lines
This marking indicates bad luck. The more lines on the individual's hand, the more bad luck they are likely to face.

Circle
A circle is a good marking to have. It indicates good luck, and protection from most troubles in life.

Square
A square signifies good protection from accidents. For example, this individual could emerge from an accident without a scratch.

Triangle
A triangle indicates an individual who possesses great inner wisdom and strength.

Grille
A grille is a negative marking here. It indicates someone who is likely to lose their luck, especially in old age.

MOUNT OF JUPITER

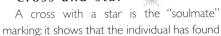

Two lines
A pair of lines indicates an individual whose ambitions are divided; they are confused over which path to follow. A line on this mount that crosses the heart line indicates that the individual is likely to suffer misfortunes in love.

Cross
The cross is a desirable marking. It indicates a very happy relationship where commitment is usually involved.

Cross and star
A cross with a star is the "soulmate" marking: it shows that the individual has found or will find their partner for life.

Star
The star marking on the mount indicates a satisfying and sudden rise to fame in life.

Square
This indicates an individual who has a natural capacity to lead or command. They may follow a military path or be a teacher.

Triangle
This marking indicates an individual who is extremely clever and diplomatic. It might be found on the palm of a successful business executive, a politician or world leader.

Grille
This marking indicates an individual who tries too hard to please.

Jupiter